NEW INVENTIONS
AND THE LATEST INNOVATIONS

....

SELF-PORTRAIT BY
GASTON DE PAWLOWSKI

NEW INVENTIONS
AND THE LATEST INNOVATIONS

Gaston de Pawlowski

INTRODUCTION BY DOUG SKINNER

TRANSLATED BY AMANDA DEMARCO

WAKEFIELD PRESS

CAMBRIDGE, MASSACHUSETTS

Wakefield Press, P.O. Box 425645, Cambridge, MA 02142

Originally published as *Inventions nouvelles et dernières nouveautés* in 1916.

Illustrations are from *Absolutely Mad Inventions,* edited by A. E. Brown and H. A. Jeffcott Jr. (New York: Dover Publications, 1970).

This book was set in Garamond Premier Pro, Helvetica Neue Pro, and American Typewriter by Wakefield Press. Printed and bound by Sheridan Saline, Inc., in the United States of America.

ISBN: 978-1-939663-98-6

Available through D.A.P./Distributed Art Publishers
75 Broad Street, Suite 630
New York, New York 10004
Tel: (212) 627-1999
Fax: (212) 627-9484

10   9   8   7   6   5   4   3   2   1

CONTENTS

INTRODUCTION

Gaston de Pawlowski was often described as larger than life: physically imposing, voluminous in his output and range of interests. As he put it, "I don't believe that a writer should specialize in the profession of writing, nor, above all, always exploit the same literary subject in the same successful form. His role is to create ideas that didn't exist before him, however modest they might be. For this, he must follow as well as he can the encyclopedic path taken by Rabelais and Voltaire, and on his return recount only the useful, new, and agreeable things of his voyage. It is the work of the writer to learn things; the reader should know only the fruit of this work."[1]

Gaston William Adam de Pawlowski (to give him his full oversized name) was born 14 June 1874 in Joigny, a commune in north-central France, in the Yonne department. His father, Albert de Pawlowski, was an engineer. His mother, Valerie de Tryon-Montalembert, left no record of interests apart from her family. As their particules indicate, both descended from noble families: he from a line of Polish counts, she from French marquis.

Gaston attended the lycée Condorcet and l'École des Sciences Politiques, with a special interest in economics. In 1897, he published his first book, *Sociologie nationale: Une définition de l'État* (National sociology: A definition of the state) describing the "Animal-State," his version of the Hobbesian Leviathan. A doctorate in economics followed, which Pawlowski later summarized: "In a doctoral thesis entitled *Philosophy of Work*, which I defended in 1901, I attempted to mark this departure between the individual and the state, showing that the identical work of a man (intellectual or physical, it doesn't matter) represents, in all civilizations, either forced labor or free labor, depending on whether it relates to the needs of the state or of the individual." A marginal note adds: "The association-state's only goal is the reduction of forced labor."[2]

This preoccupation with the individual's conflict with the Leviathan never left him. But he had already started writing lighter pieces for the new comic weekly *Le Rire*, thirty-two of which were collected by F. Juven in 1898 as *On se moque de nous* (They're making fun of us). Many of them rely on that staple of French comic literature, military life, with the misadventures of a dim-witted private called Polochon. Many more, though, are devoted to another of his favorite topics, cycling.

The bicycle was all the rage in the 1890s, and Pawlowski one of its most active promoters. He edited the weekly *Le Vélo*, was on the board of the Union vélocipédique de France, and contributed to *L'Écho des Sports de Paris*, *Vélodrôle*, *Véloce-Sport*, *La Bicyclette*, and *Paris-Vélo*. Although cycling seems to have been his favorite sport, he also enjoyed mountaineering and racing cars, and, characteristically, wrote copiously about both as well. He somehow also found time to assume the editorship of *L'Opinion*, *Automobilia*, *Spido-Journal*, and *Comœdia*, and to contribute to dozens of periodicals, among them *Le Canard Enchaîné*, *La Trompe*, *La Presse*, *L'Écho de Paris*, *L'Œuvre*, *Le Courrier français*, *Le Journal*, *Fantasio*, *Gringoire*, and *La Baïonnette*.

This outpouring of journalism was occasionally collected into books. Polochon became the hero of an eponymous (and brief) novel in 1909. Various short sketches and stories comprised *Paysages animés* (Animated landscapes), *Paysages chimériques* (Fanciful landscapes), both also from 1909, and *Contes singuliers* (Singular tales, 1918). His wartime articles were published in *Dans les rides du front* (In the wrinkles of the forehead/front, 1917) and *Signaux à l'ennemi* (Signals to the enemy, 1918), and his love of cars inspired *Ma voiture de course* (My race car, 1923). One of his last stints was as the drama critic for *Gringoire*, his final published piece being a review of André Gide's *Œdipe*. In it, he chided Gide for his mildness, compared him unfavorably to Alfred Jarry, and complained about "this low character of our era," adding: "It is because today we believe we possess a complete science of a finite world that the era is sad and joyless."[3]

This antipathy to science, or at least to scientism, was another recurring theme in Pawlowski's work. His most popular book, *Voyage au pays de la quatrième dimension* (*Voyage to the Land of the Fourth Dimension*), is fueled by it. He originally serialized this curious fantasy in *Comœdia* and *L'Auto* starting in 1909; it was then published by Librairie Charpentier Fasquelle in 1912, and expanded into its definitive edition in 1923, with elaborate illustrations by Léonard Sarluis.

Although an introductory "Examen critique" summarizes speculations about the fourth dimension, mostly taken from Charles Howard Hinton, Pawlowski is not really concerned with physics. His aim is satire, and he uses the fourth dimension as a pretext for time travel, leading to a dystopian fantasy of a future filled with everything he hated. I noted his pet peeves on my last rereading, and they form quite a list: scientism, materialism, socialism, determinism, utilitarianism, rationality, mathematics, and democracy. His pet nemesis, the Leviathan, raises its tiny but monstrous head in chapter 9: "a colossal microcephalic, superior to men and enveloping them as so many cells in its gigantic body."[4] In contrast, he champions individuality, intuition, and monarchy.

His other major work, *Inventions nouvelles et derniéres nouveautés*, appeared regularly in *Le Rire Rouge* (formerly *Le Rire*) during the war, and was collected by Fasquelle in 1916.

The imaginary invention was a well-established literary genre, with such distinguished exponents as Francis Bacon and Athanasius Kircher, and flourished even more among the technological advances of the nineteenth century. Early writers of science fiction, like Jules Verne and Albert Robida, packed their books with them; and the bohemian humorists of Montmartre, particularly Alphonse Allais and Charles Cros, delighted in coming up with fantastic inventions. Verne and Robida hoped to predict technology accurately. Allais and Cros were interested in laughs, but both had scientific backgrounds: Allais was trained as a pharmacist and patented a formula for instant coffee; Cros filed patents for an improved telegraph and a chromometer and worked on color photography and the phonograph. Pawlowski's impulse was, if not the opposite, at least different: he disliked science, and his inventions were meant to mock it.

Some of his contemporaries, notably the cartoonists W. Heath Robinson and Rube Goldberg, specialized in elaborate contraptions for simple tasks, like lighting a pipe or closing a window. Pawlowski chose another premise: a simple device that was futile or self-defeating. Allais, too, had preferred that approach, with creations like the antifilter and the kangacycle.

Later humorists were to follow suit. One of the most inventive was Jacques Carelman, who produced drawings and sculptures of "unfindable objects," such as bunk hammocks, a mechanical daisy plucker, and a snowshoe bicycle; he acknowledged his debt to Pawlowski with an illustration of the latter's bathtub outfitted with a door.[5] But there have been others: the radio comedian Colonel Stoopnagle (F. Chase Taylor) gave us holeless sieves and stationary elevators; Professeur Choron (Georget Bernier), went for the raunchy in the pages of *Hara-Kiri* or in TV spots; Al Jaffee drew meticulously plausible devices for *MAD*; Kenji Kawakami developed his "unuseless" inventions into the international pastime of chindogu, stipulating that all inventions must be impractical, not for sale, and devoid of propaganda or sexual innuendo.

There are drawbacks to the genre. One is that the inventions may prove more feasible than anticipated. Al Jaffee was bemused when his self-adhesive postage stamps and multiblade razors became reality. Kawakami never expected anyone to market his selfie stick.

Another problem is that genuine inventions may be odder than imaginary ones. Allais devoted three columns in 1901 to his discoveries in the patent files. Faced with the combination fishing pole and bicycle pump, or the summer fez, he could only remark, "Humorists who think themselves clever when they imagine dust covers for submarines, or rubber muzzles for snails to stop them dribbling on the salad, are small beer indeed next to certain serious and licensed inventors."[6]

Pawlowski's inventions were only one of his interests, but, with his usual imagination and industry, he produced a catalog of them that are both scrupulously useless and stranger than fact.

His friends and colleagues included Alfred Jarry, Tristan Bernard, Marcel Proust, and Guillaume Apollinaire. Marcel Duchamp cited *Voyage au pays de la quatrième dimension* as one of the inspirations for his *Large Glass*. And when Francis Picabia's drawings of machinery were seized by customs officials, who assumed they were plans for real machines, he called his account of the incident "Inventions nouvelles et dernières nouveautés."[7]

Pawlowski died of a heart attack on 2 February 1933. *Voyage au pays de la quatrième dimension* has remained in print, and, until now, has been his only work translated into English (by Brian Stableford, for Black Coat Press, 2009).

This edition of *Inventions nouvelles et dernières nouveautés* is long overdue. Amanda DeMarco's lively and scrupulous translation can finally introduce English readers to one of the most prolific and imaginative of all comic inventors, the Gargantuan Gaston de Pawlowski.

Doug Skinner

NOTES

1. Gaston de Pawlowski, *Polochon: Paysages animés* (Paris: La Renaissance du Livre, coll. "In Extenso," ca. 1918), 4. All translations mine.
2. Gaston de Pawlowski, *Voyage au pays de la quatrième dimension* (Paris: Eugène Fasquelle, 1923), 9.
3. *Gringoire*, 6 January 1932.

4. Pawlowski, *Voyage au pays de la quatrième dimension*, 45.

5. Carelman's illustration of Pawlowski's "baignoire à portière" can be found in his *Catalogue d'objets introuvables* (Paris: Balland, 1984), 68.

6. *Le Journal*, 25 July 1901. Allais followed this column with two other lists of improbable patents, on 31 July and 9 August.

7. *391* 1 (25 January 1917), 4.

DOUG SKINNER

PUBLISHER'S NOTE

As this first English edition of Gaston de Pawlowski's *New Inventions and the Latest Innovations* breaks with Wakefield Press's general publishing philosophy, it seemed appropriate to include a note, not so much to address what that philosophy is, but to address why I have chosen not to adhere to it for this translation and not to present the entirety of the 1916 original edition of this book (which had been a collection drawn from a range of columns Pawlowski had been writing).[1]

When publishing historical material in translation, we try to provide some degree of contextualization (introduction, afterword, endnotes), as well as present the text in accordance with the author's original intentions. The latter means maintaining a book's integrity: I prefer to avoid playing the role of impresario, selecting extracts that to my mind would constitute the "best" of an author. There are several personal reasons for avoiding this role (I am as much a reader as I am a publisher), but also practical ones; one of which is that being selective in this way can too often anchor a book to the time of its publication, and any work of interest strives to be of interest also for the long run.[2]

Maintaining integrity also means, as uncomfortable as it can sometimes be, not wearing blinders: not substituting outdated language with terms more palatable by today's standards, and not removing attitudes and stances that we'd prefer not to see displayed by or in otherwise engaging or interesting authors and books. It means, quite simply, maintaining the racism, antisemitism, sexism, and colonialism of the past. To hide such elements is, to my mind, a conservative urge and what ultimately enables a mindset today to entertain the idea that the 1950s, for example, constituted a better time to live in than the present. We publish literature of the past but have no interest in nostalgia.[3]

This project raised some quandaries, however, and highlighted the fact that retaining and maintaining outdated stances and language is easier to do with authors and works of a certain stature and influence: a novel by Joseph Conrad or Raymond Roussel offers a resilience that a more minor author or work does not (if it need be said, Wakefield Press is devoted to authors and works in what could be called a minor key), and when some offensive passages begin weighing upon the scale, a publisher can start to feel some pressure to defend its editorial decisions.

As Doug Skinner mentions in his introduction, Pawlowski's primary goal in writing, publishing, and then assembling these inventions had been for the sake of humor and satire ("the only poetry possible in our scientific era," Pawlowski here claims of humor, yet arguably the literary element that erodes most under the pressures of translation and time). While some of both are to be found in the present book (as are some offensive passages: it felt deceptive to scrub this book completely clean of discomfort for the contemporary reader), they were not the primary criteria for the final selections made here (which altogether constitute about three-quarters of the original French publication), and a loss of humorous or satirical intent over time was enough to bar an invention from inclusion if it provided no other points of interest. Some points I deemed to be of interest in this work as I decided on final selections were as follows:

ANTICIPATION: Pawlowski presents a range of inventions or innovations that, despite their satirical intent, proved to anticipate later products or ways of thinking. These include, decades before they were to see realization, Pawlowski's imagining of such things as earphones, metro-cinematic advertising, facelifts, artificial tanning, the fidget spinner, steampunk haptics, a prototype Epcot Center in the middle of Paris, the use and impact of cinematic means in warfare (half a century before Paul Virilio would fully address the topic) and other arenas, a primitive notion of biopolitics, and an unsettling rumination on the transformation of human fat into soap (here it should be noted that the myth of a German corpse factory was one that circulated during World War I).

CULTURAL ECHOES AND INFLUENCE: Assessing women in automotive terms of horsepower and suspension, for example, may not present the humor it did over a century ago, but such passages make for intriguing touchstones and parallels to some of the mechanomorphic portraits Marcel Duchamp and Francis Picabia would execute a few years later; and if Pawlowski's *Voyage to the Land of the Fourth Dimension* is often cited as the influence Pawlowski had on Duchamp, one cannot help but wonder whether the former's two-story combination revolving-door-coffee-mill in this book might not sit better alongside the latter's two-storied *Large Glass* and its incorporation of a chocolate grinder (or, alternately, Pawlowski's rigid plumb line set alongside Duchamp's *Three Standard Stoppages*). Even Pawlowski's less clever wartime "airplane traps" conjure up echoes of Max Ernst's more surreal presentations of said traps in the 1930s.

USELESSNESS: Finally, and more broadly, I made a point to maintain Pawlowski's underlying celebration of uselessness and his satirical inflation of utilitarianism to absurd extremes, especially his varied imagined means of capturing and conserving all forms of expended energy. To shake a salad instead of a hand, to harness the energy generated by a sleeping body's tossing and turning or the gravitational weight of waste products—the obsessive's urge to not let waste go to waste . . . these seemed to me to be impulses deserving of attention today more than ever.

Marc Lowenthal
Wakefield Press

NOTES

1. A decision that was also made by the publishers of the last two editions of this book in French—in 1973 from Editions Balland and in 2009 from Editions Finitude—both of which were more heavily abridged than this English translation. Interestingly, these last two abridgements in French resulted in very different books with less overlap in content than one would have expected.

2. By way of example, I was recently reading Richard Howard's 1968 edited translation of Michel Butor's two volumes of essays, *Repertoire* (published in English as *Inventory*): among the essays not included were two on modern writers deemed at the time to require too much "spadework": Raymond Roussel and Michel Leiris—the two essays our own audience today would probably be most interested in reading. Over time, margins move to the center and vice versa.

3. As to the ongoing question of whether an author can be separated from their work: no, I don't believe so. That said, and at the risk of not properly separating this author from this note, I expect authors to be flawed (at best); they are, after all, human, and only nonhuman animals fail to disappoint. But we read books, not people; it is when a book disappoints that we discard it.

NEW INVENTIONS
AND THE LATEST INNOVATIONS

PREFACE

Our readers will excuse this book's slightly coarse and necessarily scientific format. We wanted to present the public with the facts, which are certainly sometimes strange, curious, bizarre, or disconcerting, but are always investigated down to their smallest details. Of course, this work suffers from the purely documentary character of our research.

The fact is that it is no longer the time for literary reveries, but rather for practical truths. We have been reproached for coming to new ideas late in France; it has been insinuated that we aren't interested in many details of daily life where, it seems, progress is being made. It is time to act and to show that we too are capable; mere words are not enough.

Let the retrograde philosophers claim that we don't know how or why we live, that we don't understand the spirit of materiality at all, that we don't have any idea about the electricity we use every day—this is all utopian nonsense that can only impede the triumphal march of Science. Should we patiently dismantle and separately classify all the cogs in our watch, we would be astonished at the fact that, at the end of this process, we had not discovered what time it is. What does it matter to a true modern savant if he has no idea where he's going, so long as he gets there methodically?

Our elite bourgeoisie and all the conscious members of the proletariat have been seized by this desire to learn, and by this interest in all practical questions of hygiene, finance, natural science, fashion, industry, art, and literature.

I need look no further for proof than the innumerable inquiries and requests for information our five academies receive each day. Certainly, some of them of them are childish or downright absurd, but they all denote an ardent desire for knowledge and for better arming oneself for the daily battle.

Allow me to cite a few instances from the latest mail delivery:

One "Nemrod de Conflans-Sainte-Honorine" asks the Academy of Sciences if a badger can really be lured out of its den by offering it a little bowl of soap bubbles.

A society woman is astonished that, given the useful services the electric massager has provided, no one has yet thought of building an electric massagim.

A grocer is anxious to know if the sugar candy he sold legally should have been labeled "Acidic, uniquely uric."[1]

A launderer is claiming that potatoes can be used to simultaneously starch and iron collars, eliminating the need for two separate processes, and aligning laundry practices with the latest nutritional advice.

A nutritionist and contender for the Montyon Prizes would like to know if too many capers will put one at higher risk for splitting one's sides.[2]

An eagle-eyed art collector is astonished that the artist had painted a little electric locomotive rather than a steam engine on the beautiful canvas by Bruegel the Elder a dealer had sold him.

A patriot is eager to know if the height of the Great Elector of Bavaria exceeded that of most French electors.[3]

A young apprentice wonders by virtue of what ancient custom of the magistracy was "Spitting on the floor is prohibited" inscribed at the Palais de Justice.

A bank employee confirms, in his experience, it is impossible to strip a bond using gasoline.[4]

A young tenor would like to know if one can stand on the steps of an operatic scale to reach the high notes.

A wholesaler is indignant that the holes in Gruyère cheese are specially manufactured in Basel, as he was told.

A correspondent at the Academy of Humanities confirms that the thin wooden rulers which the Sybarites used to shoo flies must have been perforated to diminish air resistance.

Another informs us that the truffled foot was an ancient unit of measure in use only in the Périgord.

These are among the innumerable questions about locating the soul, photographing talent, practical utilization of the Venus de Milo, the physical labor of phantoms, braces for snakes, a machine for capturing the weather, the chemical discovery of God, and the best way to prevent people with chapped lips from laughing.

Needless to say, this inventive fever is still rather incoherent, and all of these good intentions most often lack a firm technical direction.

By describing new trends and the best inventions of our times, we wanted this volume to shape opinion and allow it to helpfully discern true from false.

By publishing certain of these inventions in advance in an important Parisian journal, we were able to see how interested the modern public is in these scientific questions. A great volume of letters attests to this.

The large export companies have repeatedly asked us to provide them with catalogs, prospectuses, and current pricing.

A livestock farmer from the north was simply enraged when I refused to give him instructions for chrome-plating his fighting cocks.

It was the Society for Animal Welfare which officially intervened in this case. Sometime before the war, there was even a big foreign magazine that enthusiastically reproduced my information concerning the new military airplane traps, which their correspondent had telegraphed to them.

Thus, we can be assured in advance that this book is of interest to those who still have much to learn but who, better advised than Bouvard and Pécuchet,[5] want to utilize science in a lucrative and practical manner, without vain humanitarian sentimentality.

Though this collection is intended for worldly neophytes with a desire to learn, we also hope that it is entertaining, if only momentarily, for those well-informed people who nonetheless would like to refresh their knowledge. Perhaps these latter will even discover a light touch of humor in certain of our descriptions that will not displease them and for which we must be pardoned.

Humor is, in effect, the only poetry possible in our scientific era, the way verse was the only open door to dreams in the prose of our fathers' time. The spirit's methods of escape vary with its prisons, and one cannot escape the absolute authoritarianism of science as easily as the despotism of bourgeois existence.

We might be reproached for amusing ourselves with "civil" questions at a moment when military problems should rank first, but a distinction must be made regarding this point.

Of course, we're aware that "civilians" currently think only of the war, but our soldiers must also be permitted to think a little about the civil life they have been defending for two years, and to draw from it as their sole source of distraction. As for war, one doesn't write it; one wages it.

Thus, it is to my comrades at the front, and to their diversion, that this book is dedicated.

G. DE P.

"... not to play, but to learn a thousand pretty tricks and new inventions, which were all grounded upon arithmetic."

RABELAIS, *Gargantua*, Vol. I, ch. XXIII

I

HYGIENE — AESTHETIC INNOVATIONS —
BEAUTY PRODUCTS

ANTI-SLIP SOAP — ADULTERINE RETICULE — TORPEDO SPITTOON — DENTURE TRAP — PESTICIDAL SALVE — ESCARFIGARO — FOR THE CONSERVATION OF THE TEETH — LIVING MOLES — TOURIST FILTER — WHISPERING MEPHISTOPHONE — ARTIFICIAL TAN — BLACK NAILS FOR THE CABARET — TIEBACKS FOR SAGGING CHEEKS — ILLUMINATION FOR THE EYES AND NOSE — LATERAL-ENTRY BATHTUB — NASAL VACUUM — IRON ELECTROFERROMATTRESS — MAMMARY SWIMMING PUMP — ALARM-CLOCK EARRINGS — CENTRAL COLLECTION SPITTOON — MIASMA STOVE — CLOSED COMB FOR THE COIFFURE-CHALLENGED — CATERPILLAR TOOTHBRUSH — GENUFLECTOL — BRAIDED SPIT-CURL FOR MONOCLES — MAGNETIC PASTE FOR METALLIC HAIR — BEARD HAIR — UMBILICAL CEMENT — HAIR SOAP — RABBIT-FAX WAX — ELDER EXTENSOR — PEDAGOGIC SHAMPOO — GRASSHOPPER SHEARS — CHIRPING CHARMS — IBIS GLOVE-OPENER — CROCODILE FORM FOR BOOTS — GENERATOR PIPE AND ELECTRIC WAISTCOAT BUTTON FOR CONVERSATION

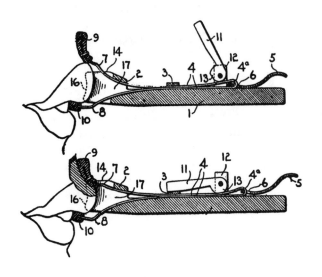

We begin this chapter by reporting on a modest invention, one without pretensions yet useful: the new *Anti-Slip Soap* is equipped with spikes and will soon make an appearance in every lavatory.

As is well known, to this day soap suffers from the grave defect of slipping between the fingers of the user and sliding on the ground with deplorable frequency. The new *Anti-Slip Soap*, analogous to the anti-skid brakes available for automobiles, eliminates all this inconvenience. It has been reported to us, incidentally, that although it cannot be used as quickly as conventional soap, it is of an appreciable quality.

The *Adulterine Reticule* is an ingenious and discreet little kit built and delivered at very affordable prices by the great London home furnishing company, Old Scratch. It can be of great service to those caught in the act of adultery. It can even—experience has proven as much—save their lives. This set, in oriental wood variegated with rich and lurid colors, contains:

Two meters of yellow silk;

A small, exotic flute;

A packet of saffron;

An instruction booklet concluding with a list of terms indicating the eventual pronunciation of some Hindu words.

The moment the chief of police knocks on the offending door, the woman, following tradition, huddles under the bedspread and her fear gives it light, spasmodic movements.

For his part, her partner in crime wastes no time in wrapping the yellow cloth around his head, arranges it in the form of a turban, hastily rubs his body with the saffron, sits cross-legged on the ground, and begins to play the flute. When, after the usual warnings, the chief of police bursts into the room, the pseudo-Hindu gives voice to plaintive protests.

"Great white chief, you not take pretty poisonous snakes of mine under blankets, only treasure to do circus tricks with."

The movements under the bedspread becoming still more pronounced with the police chief's entry, he beats a terrified retreat without any further fuss, closes the door himself, and informs the deceived gentleman that he's been the victim of a mistake. It's a simple and inexpensive apparatus at a cost not exceeding 30 francs for the current model, packaging and postage included, 35 francs for the latest model enhanced with ersatz stones.

A minor inventor from Bagnolet has just presented a new hygienic spittoon to the Academy of Medicine. Called the *Torpedo Spittoon*, its perfect cleanliness is ensured by means of a simple electric control. When one spits into this device, the spittle is immediately fired toward the ceiling with astonishing force. Thus, the device is always pristine and never requires cleaning.

Denture Traps are, we assure you, a perfectly repugnant invention attributable to our enemies, and which can never find success except among tourists or the savages on the other side of the Rhine. They are intended for business travelers or excursionists who are obliged to spend the night in country inns burgeoning with innumerable mice and rats, and who don't want these animals to disturb them during their sleep.

Denture Traps consist of a set of modern dentures which can be easily removed and then instantly returned to the mouth. They've been equipped with a simple trigger spring. Just set them on the floor in one corner of the bedroom. The wearer can then sleep in absolute tranquility. If by chance a mouse ventures into the trap, the spring releases and the jaw snaps shut, crushing the unfortunate rodent.

To bait the trap—this point we relate with extreme distaste— it is recommended tourists end their meal by eating a few nuts, dried almonds, or other such treats.

In the morning, the animal need only be removed from the trap and the spring removed. Depending on the owner's degree of propriety, the dentures can rinsed in a basin, or put directly back in the mouth.

This invention may be extremely practical and convenient, but I doubt that it will be well received among people of taste.

Some "elegant" citizens of Hamburg—always wanting to collect the greatest possible number of pelts over the course of their voyage to make a lovely fur coat—have wondered if it wouldn't be better to connect the denture traps to the hotel's electric bell system, so that the trap can be reset after each catch, allowing it to function anew.

This provision is perfectly useless because the inventor of denture traps has unfortunately foreseen this demand and created a deluxe hunting model, equipped with a pale imitation of our hydro-pneumatic artillery brake.

With this model, the denture trap bites the rat or mouse violently enough to kill the animal immediately Then the jaws slowly open and reset themselves, gaping for another capture. At a country inn, eight to ten rats per night can be caught in this way, but not more, as the force of denture traps decreases with each bite.

Pesticidal Salve is a new paste in a lovely golden color which can be slathered on bald heads, and which is sold, ready for application, in quarter-liter bottles complete with brush for 2.25 francs, in all the best pharmacies. *Pesticidal Salve* is analogous to the paste applied to flypaper. Its effect is deadly. Anyone with a bald head who knows how intolerable it is in summer to feel countless flies walking across the smooth surface of one's skull will understand the joy of capturing these irritating insects and sparing one's neighbors their annoyance. This devotion to the common good is one of the chief attributes of a family man. He is the true guardian of the household. When his head is completely covered in flies, a simple wash suffices to remove his striking black toupee. Let us add that the producer of the *Pesticidal Salve* sells a deluxe paste which contains flakes of gold, marvelously resembling aventurine. Applied to the skull, its effect is striking. For grand weddings, a palette of premium-quality pastes is available, giving the delightful impression of lacquerwork.

The *Escarfigaro* is a new safety razor, offering tremendous advantages to tourists, business travelers, and explorers.

It is a large snail, Australian in origin, which secretes a soapy slime when placed on a cheek bristling with beard. Once the face is covered in this soap foam, the bearded man in question need only press down on the snail, which curls up into the far reaches of its abode, allowing the edges of its shell to take on the function of an excellent razor; these edges are, in fact, particularly sharp. One can shave with them in a matter of minutes, without difficulty and without carrying any cumbersome equipment on one's person.

The *Escarfigaro* is sold in a small wire-mesh box, with a bit of soapwort to feed it. It also makes a charming little travel companion. It can be found in all the best pharmacies.

In scientific circles, everyone is talking about a new method which allows anyone to keep their own teeth clean and white forever, even at an advanced age. This method is infinitely simple, and it's astonishing that no one has recommended it sooner. Instead of waiting for the teeth to deteriorate with age, one simply has to pull them out in early youth, when they begin to grow, and then mount them as dentures. Thus, *one's own teeth can be kept clean and perfectly healthy forever*. It presents a serious advantage that will be appreciated by all those unfortunates who are obliged to accept false teeth culled from the mouths of others.

Yet another American trend is set to sweep our beaches. But will it really be accepted? One must hope not, because if it satisfies the eccentric tastes of the transatlantics, it can only injure the natural finesse of the Latin races. I'm referring to the new *Living Mole*, which those elegant denizens of New York affix to their cheeks with one foot, just next to their mouths. It seems that this induces extremely "exciting" sensations, and signifies, through a bit of rather coarse symbolism, that this charming mouth can be approached without fear. A far cry from delightful beauty marks of our grandmothers! One can only hope, we repeat, that this absurd eccentricity will find no success on French soil.

Presenting a new *Tourist Filter*, which promises to deliver the greatest of benefits. It's a sort of felt plug equipped with a cord. Once swallowed, the plug rests in the esophagus, while the user is free to drink water of dubious origin.

Once the tourist is quenched, a tug on the cord is all that is required to extract the improvised filter from his throat. Of modest volume, the filter takes up little space in the traveler's pocket.

The *Whispering Mephistophone* is a curious little invention which is certainly destined to find considerable success. Hardly had its existence been announced when orders flowed in from everywhere. This device, simple as it is ingenious, consists of a specially shaped little phonograph which is concealed in the hair and whose receivers end discreetly at the ears, passing under the hair or the strap of

GASTON DE PAWLOWSKI

a hat. A bit of cotton in the ears will easily conceal the two small tubes. According to the client's wish, the *Mephistophone* whispers either bawdy tunes or romantic sentiments. Its words are only perceptible to the wearer of the device. Thus, one can make every moment agreeable, whether in church—whence the name of the device—at formal events, or when attending poetry salons. It would be wrong to tax these little aides-to-immorality, as one is at first inclined, since they prevent the wearer, particularly young girls, from listening to real romantic sentiments and providing them with a diversion whose consequences are ultimately less dire. Since this little device was invented, innumerable deliveries have been made—in an extremely discreet manner, what's more—in the most diverse milieus. A particularly large number are sent to married women subject to discussions of housekeeping and magistrates who must endure interminable appointments. There is no doubt about its success. It is highly warranted in the boring epoch in which we live.

The Tanpath, despite its somewhat pretentious title, is a beauty product that will be appreciated by all our most elegant citizens. This dye, applied to the skin, gives those who haven't been able to leave Paris the exact tone of a tourist returning from the mountains or the sea. Thus, everyone's pride is secured.

The *Ochre Yellow* model, for returning from the trenches, is available for men.

Of interest to elegant individuals who wish to frequent the wildest cabarets, the new *Black Celluloid Nail Crescents* can be affixed easily under the nails and removed with the same ease. Upstanding people are always recognizable by the fact that they have clean nails. The black celluloid nail crescents make everything clear in a matter of seconds.

This winter certain milliners intend to release *Tiebacks for Sagging Cheeks*. The ensemble, it seems, is exceedingly elegant and will be the delight of all coquettes of a certain age.

The American Fashion Convention has decided to replace conventional jewelry, which lacks a certain éclat, with electrical jewelry, which will have more of an effect. We hasten to add that the innovation goes even further, extending the charms of one's natural physiognomy. Thus, the Americans have already constructed new arched velvet eyebrows which rest on the existing brows and contain small electric tubes, analogous to those found in piano lamps and which are illuminated by means of mercury vapors. This light, which is completely invisible from the exterior, is projected onto the eyes of the wearer, lending his or her eyes a truly stunning brilliance.

Also to be highlighted are the little electric nasal bulbs, which are concealed in the nose, giving the end of the nose an extremely seductive rosy transparency. Electric dentures have recently made it possible for the wearer to offer a dazzling smile. I'm well aware that certain parties won't hesitate to protest against these Yankee inventions, but as is always the case with new inventions, we shall adopt them in the end.

For periods of excessive heat, I am overjoyed to present the new *Lateral-Entry Bathtub*, constructed by a leading plumbing firm. We all know how exhausting it is to step over the side of a bathtub to get into the water or to get out, especially in hot weather. Thanks to the new lateral entrance, one merely opens a little door to enter the bathtub on level footing.

For all those fashionistas eager not to spoil their coiffure, the new little pocket *Nasal Vacuum* can be concealed in a bag or cuff and allows the user to blow her nose discreetly and without pushing aside her veil by inserting the little vacuum into the nose via one of the openings in the tulle. It's elegant, practical, and discreet.

All those among us who have lived in a barracks are familiar with the enchanting custom of *changing the mattress straw*. Theoretically, as is widely known, this consists of the monthly renewal of the straw which fills the interior of the soldier's sack. In fact, they usually make do with swapping straw with a neighboring bed. This exchange has the positive effect of driving off a certain number of bedbugs, but it is absolutely ineffective for ensuring the complete destruction of these parasites.

As of next year, the military bed administration will instate a costly but dynamic reform. The plant-based straw in military beds will be replaced with steel wool, which is just as soft, and which allows for the total destruction of these parasites using a radical method. As of now the administration refers to this new procedure under the somewhat pompous name of *electroferromattress*, while our troops refer to it more familiarly as the electro. Every month, a strong electric current will be sent through each military mattress, instantly electrocuting all those nefarious animals in the bedding. It's fast, simple, ingenious, inexpensive, and provides antiseptic benefits to please the most rigorous of our hygienists.

Here we have a small item for the feminine toilette that will be all the rage on our beaches this year. It's the *Mammary Swimming Pump*, manufactured by a pneumatic inflatables firm, which will provide the greatest advantages to all our lovely bathers. This little instrument is just an elegant simplification of the current model's air pump. It can be easily carried along in a suitcase or even in a simple bag. Equipped with a special rubber connector called the "universal connector," it can adapt to any valve, and serves to inflate ladies' bosoms before bathing. Once filled, they can be used to rest effortlessly on the water or to learn how to swim. There is absolutely nothing indelicate about this proposition. To the contrary, it grants an advantageous appearance to ladies who have not been favored by nature. The *Mammary Swimming Pump* can also be used to great advantage in case of a shipwreck, rendering unnecessary the troublesome and always risky search for a life vest. Recent experiments with wet nurses have even permitted us to observe that these women, inflated only to two atmospheres, could support up to eight people grasping onto them in the water. This is a virtual revolution in seafaring. To close, we would like to address a mundane concern: if their mistresses prefer not to leave them on the shore, nothing prevents small dogs from being rendered similarly unsinkable when bathing, allowing them to frolic joyously and without danger in the sea.

To summarize, this is an extremely simple and practical invention whose success is assured.

We are all familiar with the wristwatch, and those little minuscule stopwatches they seem to be putting everywhere these days in place of the gemstones on jewelry. A jeweler has taken it upon himself to improve on this useful invention, creating the extremely ingenious *Alarm-Clock Earrings*. In place of diamonds these earrings hold two little alarm clocks whose ringing can be adjusted in intervals of just a few minutes, to assure a perfect start to the morning. These new pieces of jewelry will be welcomed by travelers who fear sleeping too late and missing their train.

In recent years, the hotel industry has made truly prodigious efforts; the material organization of a modern grand hotel is a far cry from those inns of yesteryear. Central heating, electricity, telephone, rotary machines for printing hotel invoices—they've thought of everything. A modern palace is an immense clock assembled with great care down to the tiniest gear.

Would you like to have a glimpse of one of these tiny improvements, which amount to nothing at first glance, and yet which show just how far the concern for organization extends in these enormous modern palaces? We need only present the new *Central Collection Spittoon*, which has been installed almost everywhere for the start of the season. Many people consider it to be an insignificant detail, or merely a repugnant one. That doesn't reflect well on their scientific spirit, for there's nothing insignificant or repugnant about it for the truly learned.

The *Central Collection Spittoon* is a welcome replacement for the current hideous little spittoon, which is so often the site of tiresome accidents when all the sawdust has been eaten away by *inattentive external rumination*, as a physician might put it, giving it a most disagreeable appearance. With the *Central Collection Spittoon*, all of that is history. Each hotel room is outfitted with an elegant little spittoon-funnel, which ends in a small tube descending into a central drainage system. This drainage system extends below ground, into the little room dedicated to the polishing of boots, and terminates in a small faucet. You can guess the rest. In the morning, the unfortunate salaried employee charged with polishing hundreds of hotel boots need no longer make those desperate and heroic salivary efforts, often so disastrous for his health. He must only occasionally open the little faucet placed at his disposition. By ridding themselves of their excess saliva in a hygienic fashion, the residents of the hotel effortlessly provide for the daily polishing of their shoes. It's infinitely cleaner, more discreet, and more humane to the poor boot-polishing employees, whose delight at the improvement is a pleasure to behold.

Let us add, by way of conclusion, that this invention will soon be adopted in all our barracks and boarding schools and that the ministries of education and of war have already appointed two commissions tasked with studying the results presented.

Tenants, watch out! In place of costly heating, certain unscrupulous landlords have decided to use *swamp miasmas*, which are spread via the heating system, giving inhabitants a light fever and consequently the illusion of warmth. This is a fraudulent practice, let us remember, punishable by law.

In the domain of fashion, we would like to draw your attention to the new *Closed Comb for the Coiffure-Challenged*. One often notices how absurd it is for completely bald individuals to use an ordinary comb whose teeth are divided. The closed comb, by contrast, polishes the head for a more desirable effect which, rather than uselessly scratching the skull, gives it the gleaming quality of antique ivory.

Is it known to what the Negroes of the Haut-Tamba owe their dazzlingly white teeth? An English explorer has explained it to us in the most recent issue of the English scientific journal, *The Scalp*.

Every morning these Negroes take one of those big caterpillars bristling with hair, very commonly found in the country, which they roll in dental powder and then place on their close-fitted teeth, imprisoning them there by closing their mouths. The caterpillar, which is panicked by the dental powder, squirms in every direction, passes over all the teeth in seeking a way out; it tries to squeeze through all the gaps, and in a few minutes, the teeth are thoroughly cleaned. All that's needed then is to spit out the caterpillar, which proceeds to wash itself in the neighboring stream.

Not without good reason is it said: everything is a matter of prejudice, and this method, which seems utterly repugnant to us in France, is the one most used among the natives of Haut-Tamba.

"Is it out of bias," George Auriol[6] wrote to me, "that you keep silent about *Genuflectol*, which makes the knees of camels flexible so they will kneel?"

No, it's certainly not out of bias, because I am aware of the marvelous properties of Genuflectol, as it is currently used among courtesans in the courts of African kings. It is only that I am aware of my scientific responsibilities and the disastrous applications that have been undertaken with Genuflectol. By a regrettable error several years ago, the heads of certain members of the institute were anointed with the substance. Their knees were suddenly relaxed, then stiffened, and softened again in the course of our session, and the dignity of our assembly was diminished.

At the same time, I remember the marvelous effects that one of our most distinguished professors of music derived in days gone by from the use of Genuflectol for the instruction of his students. The good fellow had a face that was as deeply lined as a musical staff, and at the same time afflicted by a number of beauty marks. Thanks to Genuflectol, his face became mobile, furrowed itself at will, raising or lowering the little notes formed by the beauty marks. And this is how the fellow composed, instinctively, the musical themes that his students, crowded around him, played immediately and with admiration. But this is an exceptional case, only of interest, as it were, to historians of music.

The new developments in fashion this year seem to be focused particularly on hair. On the heels of this trend, this summer we are hailing the introduction of the sponge wig, which can be soaked in cool water during hot spells, or even in ether, according to the preference of the wearer. Hairdressers have also asked us to alert their male clientele that to be elegant, they must allow the hair over their temples to grow out. Soon, it will be the style to wear a plaited spit-curl that serves as a monocle chain. Only elegant, fashionable men will be ready to take part in this trend immediately.

Speaking of hairstyles, we would also like to report that green shall be the stylish hair color next year. It is the complementary color to red, and so your hairstyle will harmonize more completely with your lips and cheeks. At least insofar as one does not opt for green lips and red hair. Milliners have not yet announced fashions for next season to suit that trend.

Still on the topic of hairstyles, we must draw your attention to the ingenious *Magnetic Paste*, with which the most notorious bald pates among us are slathered. One must then simply bring artificial wire hair in proximity with the skull, which is attracted by the magnetic paste and immediately sticks to the head. Thus, the artificial hair naturally takes its place on the living skin of the skull. For military men who desire a crew cut, ordinary nails should suffice.

And finally, we would like to add, for ladies fond of yellow dyes, that the wire hairs soon display a lovely rust color after just a few washes.

Each day the marvels of modern surgery astonish us anew. Now a new and truly surprising operation has been announced, capable of causing hair to regrow. No longer are we interested in mysteriously formulated lotions and long-term treatments, but rather a surgical procedure with immediate results. It has long been noted that most bald men have full beards. By means of delicate ligatures and silk threads passed through the head, each beard hair is connected to a hair root on the scalp. Once this has been accomplished, placing progressive tension on the new hair causes the beard hair to move from the chin to the scalp. After that, the patient is free to shave in the American style. This treatment may at first seem a bit hair-raising, long, and painstaking, but it offers surprising results, and only the technicians will be able to guess that the patient's hairs are from his beard. The illusion is perfect.

The new *Umbilical Cement* released by a large perfumer seems less useful to me. It appears that having a navel is totally out this winter. Could this result in significant health problems? I believe it is advisable to consult with doctors before blindly adopting this crazy trend.

Hair Soap is a new soap which will be the joy of tourists, and motorists in particular. It looks like an ordinary bar of soap, but in reality, it unites two toiletry accessories that are indispensable for washing one's hands: the *soap* of course, and *the brush*. As indicated by its name, hair soap includes hairs mixed into the soap, which allow the hands to be brushed while they are being washed.

The strange part about this invention from an industrial point of view is its very low production price. In fact, they are made of the concentrated soap suds collected from beards at barbershops after clients have been shaved.

We can't recommend strongly enough that all hunters soften their boots with the new *Rabbit-Fat Wax*, which provides the best results. After a long chase across the fields, when the tired hunter rests in the shade of an oak, his devoted dog, attracted by the scent of rabbit, will begin to enthusiastically lick his boots, which will immediately be rendered perfectly clean.

It's a kind treat for man's faithful companion and, at the same time, for his faithful wife, who will no longer go into a frenzy tearing apart their domicile because he has dirty feet.

The *Elder Extender* is a very practical device whose use poses no danger and which, unlike analogous surgical interventions intended for beautifying the elderly, is approved by the Academy of Medicine.

In principle, the Elder Extender resembles the shoe trees inserted into boots to preserve their original form and to remove the wrinkles that appear with use in the leather. At night, it is inserted in the elder's mouth, expanding the cheeks by means of a central screw with which it is adjusted to the desired size. The mouth must remain firmly closed, supported by an elastic bandage around the jaw. The path of the screw is generally cleared by means of a false removable tooth, which is removed at night when inserting the Extender. Breathing occurs unobstructed through the nose, and the next morning, the elder's face has an appearance of repose and youth which recalls that of the little chubby-cheeked angels one sees in paintings at churches.

The *Elder Extender* is available in all sizes, within the deviation of the screw, following the placement of false teeth. It is delivered in a case, ready for insertion.

An analogous but more elegant model is available for ladies. Since ladies generally have a complete set of dentures, it consists of a rubber balloon, which automatically inflates in the mouth by means of a highly ingenious *tooth valve*. This tooth valve allows air to enter but not to escape. When she closes her jaw, air pressure inside the mouth is increased, causing the tooth valve to act as a pneumatic pump, inflating the balloon inside. This device has one great advantage: it can be kept discreetly in the mouth all day without attracting attention, since beautiful women generally have nothing to say. Let us add that at mealtime the balloon can be easily deflated by pressing on the tooth valve with a simple toothpick.

The Municipal Council has decided to have an *Automobile Pit* dug in the courtyard of every elementary school. The children will be gathered in the pit each morning with only their heads emerging above ground level. The headmaster need only call over a street sweeper vehicle, and in just a few seconds all their heads will have gotten a thorough shampooing.

Speaking of hair, do you know how the natives of central Africa cut their hair? They simply put a handful of crickets in a wooden bowl and turn it upside down over their heads. In less than a quarter of an hour, all their hair is trimmed down to the scalp. They then remove the bowl, and the crickets fly away.

It's practical and affordable.

It frequently comes to pass, particularly at formal balls, that gallant gentlemen discreetly pinch those *false feminine charms*, which women wear here and there under their clothing these days, and which give them the favored appearance that cruel mother nature has denied them. This doesn't lead to any grave harm for the lady, who of course can't feel a thing. If she's an honest woman, her indifference will seem suspicious. If she's disreputable, then she's missing out on a chance for an adventure.

The *Chirping Charms* is a very simple little musical device placed inside of those false charms, be they on the bosom or the rear, and which produces a marvelous imitation of the cry emitted by any young lady upon being pinched. Thus, the chirping charms simultaneously warns the overly gallant gentleman as well as the lady who is the object of his pursuits. It is indispensable to a well-considered modern wardrobe.

A new fashion has been brought back by Parisians who winter in Egypt; it will surely be all the rage this season. It's the *Domestic-Ibis Glove-Opener*. I fear that any description of it is useless. The *Ibis Glove-Opener* functions just like the *scaly Little Crocodile Shaper for Hunting Boots*. One need only show the animal a treat after sticking its beak in one finger of a glove. Immediately, the ibis opens its beak, and the glove along with it. It's extremely simple and enhances the decor of any powder room.

While we're on the topic, let us recall how the *Crocodile Shaper for Hunting Boots* functions, for those who may not be aware. This invention is familiar to any Egyptian: one sticks the head of a small crocodile into the boot and recites a few verses of the Qur'an to it. Of course, the little crocodile begins to yawn, enlarging the boot as intended. The great advantage of the crocodile is that its snout is covered in irregularly placed scales. Simply choose a little crocodile whose scales protrude where the wearer has a callus from the shoe. The boot will thus be perfectly shaped according to its owner's foot. All Egyptian bootmakers possess a complete series of little crocodiles with differently arranged scales, to suit their various clients' needs.

An engineer wrote to me to suggest a method for recovering the energy wastefully lost in pipes from the combustion of their tobacco. According to him, a simple steam-producing coil could drive a little generator, which in turn would charge a battery. This kindly inventor estimates that the whole outfit wouldn't weigh more than ten kilos. That may be a lot for a pipe, but, as he judiciously observed, it's very little for a power plant.

It seems to me, without wanting to contest the value of this invention, that one could simply make use of the force of the breath in the mouthpiece of the pipe to drive the generator directly. How could the energy thus recovered be utilized, you ask me? Why, in a thousand different ways!

First, it could be used to illuminate foreign-won military decorations at night. In an age when abominable scheming has thoughtlessly discredited various exotic orders, it would be good to do something for the people who bear them, and to give them some compensation.

The decoration would, of course, be made of colored glass and illuminated from within, making it tasteful and discreet.

One could also use the energy recovered by the generator pipe to drive a little electric alarm which would sound continuously when an interlocutor, caught up in the heat of conversation, grabbed you by the lapel. At first, this walking annoyance won't be bothered by the alarm, but eventually, when he hears it go off each time he touches your lapel, a connection between these two facts cannot help but form in his mind, which he'll find disconcerting. Of course, *politesse* demands that the gentleman with the alarm system on his lapel remain impassive throughout the conversation, seemingly unaware of this little alarm, which is electrical and discreet in character.

II

HORTICULTURE – POULTRY –
PISCICULTURE – LIVESTOCK

PISCINE AIR LEVEL – FLOUNDER COMBS – TOURING CLUB BENCH
FOR SARDINES – MAKEUP FOR WRINKLED APPLES – NATURAL
SPONGE TOWEL – ICHTHYOCINEMA – COWS WITH SWEETENED MILK
– PROSTHETIC LEGS FOR SHEEP – CRUTCHES FOR CICADAS – ROLLERS
FOR SNAILS – DINING CARS FOR SPARROWS – CARAMELIZED FLEAS
FOR DOGS – COFFEE COWS AND BEER COWS – BOGIE BASSET HOUND
– MOTORIZED PLANING MACHINE FOR HEADS OF COD – TURBINE-
DRIVEN RACEHORSE – CHROME-PLATED FIGHTING COCKS – SAINT
FRANCIS TOP HAT – PEARL-PRODUCING MUSSELS – PEARL-
PRODUCING MUSCLES – PEARL-SEDUCING MUSSELS – WHISTLE-
MUSSELS – PEARLS FOR HARES–PEARLS FOR GIRLS – SNARL-
PRODUCING MUSSELS – CHISEL-MUSSELS – AVIAN EXPLOSIONS
– STORKS FOR CURLING ENDIVE – MONOCLES FOR HORSES – THE
OVIDATUM POULTRY MARKER – FRUIT BELLS – CONFORMATOR
FOR SQUARE EGGS – HINGES FOR BULLDOGS – WATERFOWL EGGS
FOR CARNIVAL CANNONS – THE AMBUSH – THE MUCUS MARATHON

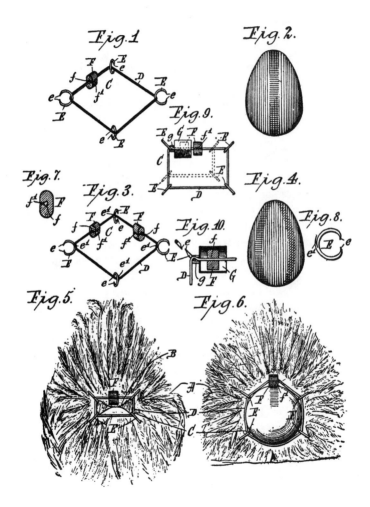

Fig.1.

Fig.2.

Fig.9.

Fig.7.

Fig.3.

Fig.10.

Fig.4.

Fig.8.

Fig.5.

Fig.6.

Very curious studies are currently underway at the museum concerning the equilibrium of fish. We now know that fish have a sense of equilibrium in the water thanks to a bubble of air which shifts along the course of their spinal column, exactly like a water level. The bubble causes a tickling sensation, sometimes toward the head, sometimes toward the tail, allowing the fish to rectify its horizontal positioning. Significantly, if a fish imprudently positions itself vertically, with its mouth pointed toward the surface of the water, the bubble of air escapes.

Now here is something even more curious: one wonders how the flounder can keep itself so perfectly perpendicular in the water, given that its port is somewhat larger than its starboard. Why, in a word, does the flounder not founder? This is because, apparently, the skeleton of the flounder takes the form of a fine-toothed comb. In other words, it is a highly upright, meticulous fish. *It is the presence of this comb that gives the flounder the right to right itself.* This observation will soon be the object of a significant report to the Academy of the Sciences.

The Touring Club of France has made a gift of six new benches for Breton fishermen. These benches are placed at pleasant sites along the coast, just a few meters from the water, in the hope that they will attract large numbers of sardines to our coasts.

Will the refinements of luxury ever know an end? We've just received a leaflet from a doctor in Bern, Professor Otto Taxis, who promises he can return old, wrinkled apples to their original firmness with his vibrating massage device. In two sessions, it seems, the wrinkles will be removed from old apples, rendering them tableworthy without further ado.

Recently at the Academy of Sciences, some very odd specimens of the *Natural Sponge Towel* were presented, which had recently been collected in the great fisheries of Ceylon. Until now, *sponge towels* were merely vulgar cotton imitations of natural sponge.

To obtain a *True Sponge Towel*, one must dive to the bottom of the sea, where young sponges have been imprisoned in enormous black chambers in order to develop. Beneath the door of the underwater enclosure, the cultivator must take pains to leave an opening precisely the thickness of the sponge towel he hopes to obtain. Quite naturally, the sponge grows bored of its dark room, and reaches for the light, stretching little by little under the door. The diver must simply cut off the desired length to obtain a *Natural Sponge Towel*. A second sponge will also grow via the hole of the door lock, which can be harvested for sponge-based cotton swabs. It's clearly ingenious, though the production price of the towel is extremely high.

GASTON DE PAWLOWSKI

Fishermen are thrilled. Thanks to *Ichthyocinema*, they can carry out impressive fishing trips.

This cinema is placed on a fishing boat, and at night it projects images into the deep waters capable of delighting even the most unimaginative of fish. Fifteen hundred meters of film spool past the joy-widened eyes of the aquatic race, including views of old pieces of Gruyère full of worms, decomposing cuts of meat, and an entire teeming world of insects. The fish, delighted, come from all over, and when the fishermen haul in the nets, it resembles a second miraculous catch of fish.

Different films can be played to suit the tastes of various fish. A great variety of images is available to nocturnal fishing amateurs.

A note for livestock feeders: according to a recent report presented to the Academy of Medicine, cows can be fed exclusively beetroot to obtain excellent *Sweetened Milk* that can be sold for 15 instead of 10 cents per cup.

Don't throw away your *leg-of-mutton sleeves*, oxidized or faded though they may be—the Society for the Protection of Animals implores you. What you may not know is that each year the S.P.A. rushes hundreds of old leg-of-mutton sleeves to the Alps each year, which provide instant aid to migrating sheep that have broken a leg on their difficult annual voyage.

The broken leg is cut off right away and sold to a local restaurant. The leg-of-mutton sleeve can be secured to the sheep with a setscrew, allowing the beast to continue on its way immediately.

When it is slaughtered for the table, mutton with a sleeve has a higher value because of its appealing culinary presentation, proving the sleeve to be a benefit to everyone.

Jitès jamaï vostri viého alliimetto! "Don't throw away your old matches!" Thus the leading Occitanian societies of the south implore us, and I hardly know of a more moving sentiment than that which inspires our excellent Provençals to their cry for charity. Specifically, they would like to provide help to elderly cicadas disabled by age and infirmity, who drag themselves onerously through the fields. Provided with used matches, the cicadas and grasshoppers can make themselves the crutches they need to walk. Because of their rounded form and elasticity, wax matches are particularly in demand. It's a poet's idea that only poets could enact.

Inspired by the touching example of these Félibristes,[7] Burgundian folk have started an analogous campaign. After a hot summer, it seems that snails completely run out of the slime with which they move along the ground, and so they dry up in place. For them, wax matches would be invaluable as rollers. It's an important undertaking, which cannot help but deeply touch animal lovers.

Every Parisian has surely noticed those lovely little dung tricycles which circle the grand boulevards, gathering praise from the public along with the scant digestive waste left by our rapid but unretentive steeds. However, this invention has the drawback of snatching food from the mouths of the poor birds, and the Society for the Protection of Animals is concerned by the state of things. Thus, the tricycle's receptacle will be transformed into a bird feeder where little birds can alight. Isn't this an invention worthy of our century of speed and progress, these little *Dining Cars for Sparrows* rolling down our avenues at 30 kilometers per hour?

Among the small inventions currently cropping up among the better veterinarians, we must mention the boxes of *Caramelized Fleas* covered in crystallized sugar, which sell for the very reasonable price of ten cents. The *Caramelized Fleas* are placed in puppies' fur to teach them to eagerly search for any fleas that might be there, and which they'll henceforth view as candy. This modest invention will be very much appreciated by dog breeders and trainers everywhere.

One recalls the triumphal welcome offered by the Academy of Medicine some time ago when the new *Coffee Cows* were presented. Bred with the old milk cows, these new ruminants were to ensure that the French population received a healthy, nourishing breakfast of indisputable quality.

Today the scales have fallen from our eyes. It was indeed somewhat surprising to see cows produce coffee instead of milk, but in those first moments of enthusiasm, our scientists failed to examine the question further. Today the mystery has come to light. The livestock farmers only fed their cows chicory, and so the coffee they produced was of inferior quality.

In terms of progress, it has once again been demonstrated that we can't try to push things too quickly.

As for the much-discussed German *Beer Cows*, today everyone knows the score and they've thankfully quit pushing this odious German invention on us.

Many hunters have written to me urgently requesting information on the new *Bogie*[8] *Basset Hounds* they've seen on offer in the brochure of a Belgian breeder. Let's clear things up right away. *Bogie Basset* is just a made-up term invented by the breeder, and I needn't tell you that the basset is not equipped with two chassis with four wheels each, like a dining car. No, the matter is much simpler, but no less curious. Truly incredible progress has been made in transplant technology for animals. It is now possible to transplant two paws to the middle of the basset's body, allowing it to hug curves of a gentle radius despite its length, and to maneuver without difficulty in complicated burrows. This six-pawed basset is originally from Holland. It was initially constructed to cross the canal bridges, which are pitched at a rather steep angle, and at whose apex the poor dogs would frequently become suspended in equilibrium at their midpoint.

They've really got the wrong idea in Paris, which has provoked veritable riots among the Breton fishermen of Newfoundland. As always, these interminable discussions revolve around new mechanical progress which simplifies labor and replaces, always for the better, the man with the machine.

This time, all the trouble started with one invention, excellent in and of itself, which the Americans have just introduced in Newfoundland. It's the *New Motorized American Ice Planing Machine for Heads of Cod.* Those unfamiliar with modern methods of cod fishing will undoubtedly be astounded by the name alone. It will be a revelation for those unfortunate inhabitants of the Breton coast who haven't yet seen the new machine at work.

The peaceable Parisian fishermen imagine that one angles for cod with simple bait or a net. They have no idea how much time that would take to catch all the cod shipped to us each year. Perhaps they haven't even noticed the systematic absence of heads on the cod which arrive in Europe?

The method employed to catch these valuable fish is at once exceedingly ingenious, exceedingly simple, and—need I say it?—exceedingly obscure. It's based on the mysterious seductive effect which the sound of the accordion, and all music, has on the cod.

The captains of cod fishing vessels wait with care, thermometer in hand, for the moment when the sea is about to freeze in the area around Newfoundland. At this moment a most wonderful music can be heard rising from all the boats, and the cod raise their heads slightly above water by the thousands. There they remain, listening, without taking notice of the ice forming on the surface of the sea which will soon imprison them. It's mere child's play for our Breton countrymen to mow down, like a field of buckwheat, all the cod heads sticking out of the ice. However, you must understand that it would take many long days of work to bring this process to a successful conclusion and then to pull up the immobilized bodies of the cod like so many beetroots.

The new *Motorized American Ice Planing Machine for Heads of Cod* accomplishes this same work in just a few hours, thus depriving the Breton mowers of their daily bread for the season.

It's an intolerable situation, which the government must address immediately. We in France have always neglected the question of Newfoundland; our diplomats regret it. Here is an occasion to intervene, which will make our ministers particularly popular among maritime voters.

Out of sheer curiosity, we draw your attention to an unlikely experiment recently undertaken at an American racetrack by a horse mounted with an airplane propeller. It was a cruel attempt which justly outraged various progressive societies the world over, and which we can be sure has no future.

The *Aero-Pegasus* was equipped, as all the American newspapers reported, with a gas turbine which drove a propeller mounted, well, in the horse's rear axis. Its braided tail helped hold the turbine in place.

Before the race, they forced the poor thoroughbred to consume six kilos of calcium carbide, and at the starting line they had him drink a bucket of water, producing a tremendous amount of gas. It was an appalling spectacle, heartrending and ridiculous at once; I shan't dwell on it. The speeds attained were undeniably prodigious, but I need not describe to you in what condition the unfortunate horse arrived at the finish line. He died in agony some hours later. Frankly, this sort of cruelty may entertain sporting men for a moment, but science must condemn it mercilessly.

The excitement elicited in the north following the introduction of *Chrome-Plated Cocks* still hasn't subsided. As is well known, the skin of these fighting cocks is completely impervious to attack, upending the habitual conditions of combat. One curious detail in this regard: the eye alone can't undergo the indispensable preparations to fight, and so farmers must harden their fighting cocks by other means if they are to give them a sufficiently imposing gaze. But these are barbarous games of another age and cannot truly interest our modern scientists.

Many people who spend their days at the window watching passersby have asked me for information on the new top hat whose base has been replaced by a bird's nest.

This hat, called the *Padded Stovepipe*, has long been worn by the most influential members of the Society for the Protection of Animals. They're worried about the dismal fate of birds in large cities where the adoption of central heating has greatly reduced the number of warm chimneys on Parisian roofs. Under these sad conditions, the poor little birds die of cold in winter, deprived of the gentle heat of our city's chimneys. How to address this danger? With a method as simple as it is heroic: tear open top hats, offering the birds a warm, padded shelter suspended over our heads.

The little sparrows and swallows immediately understood this gesture. They come to nest and to incubate their eggs on the heads of their heroes. What's more, this new stovepipe, called the *Saint Francis* by hatters, is perfectly elegant. Worn by a tall enough man, it retains a civilized appearance. It's all the better if now and again a little sparrow head mischievously pops up to regard the world outside the nest. It all owes to the perspicacity of some idle retirees who introduced this touching practice.

We complete our report with information on certain bald members of the Society for the Protection of Animals who, by means of a little periscope, have installed a mirror allowing the bird to constantly observe the skull beneath it. This view causes it to lay enormous eggs, and the skull itself replaces the plaster egg one generally places in nests.

On our Norman coasts there is great excitement surrounding the first trials of the *Pearl-Producing Mussel*. It seems one need only place a false pearl inside the mussel. Immediately beside itself with excitement, in a few weeks it secretes a pretty little pearl which looks, more or less, like the pearl of an oyster. This would amount to a veritable fortune for our Norman fishermen. On top of this, at naval bases, the mussels which have remained on the old brass hulls and are dangerous to eat would produce treasures fit to be called the pearls of the orient.

These *Pearl-Producing Mussels* remind us of an amusing anecdote. When it was announced at the Academy of Sciences, a small provincial journal modestly entitled the *Farmer's Informer* reproduced this information in a truly unforeseen fashion. Undoubtedly owing to a transcription error, the agricultural editor of this journal printed it as *Pearl-Producing Muscles*, and you can imagine the uproar caused by this departmental folly! According to this article, a diet rich in oysters, combined with regular physical exertion, can result in a physique that will delight your sweetheart in more ways than one. An interesting detail: one supposedly need only inject a grain of sand beneath the skin of a properly nourished muscle to produce this effect. But let's return to serious matters.

With regard to *Pearl-Producing Mussels*, it seems that to obtain good results, a false pearl isn't necessarily needed. One must only stimulate the mussel by piercing a little hole in its shell, and these holes can be made very rapidly with a sewing machine. Mussels pricked by a machine immediately secrete nacre around the hole, producing pretty pearls. However, certain greedy cultivators introduced too many holes and the mussels contented themselves with making waistcoat buttons, which is, one must admit, a lesson and an example.

We should also mention a new invention in the same category as *Pearl-Producing Mussels*, and more realistic than *Pearl-Producing Muscles*, which I think is destined to cause quite a stir.

It is the new breed of *Pearl-Seducing Mussel*, currently used by Norman fishermen to expedite pearl harvesting. These mussels are more aggressive than either ordinary or pearl-producing mussels, and they are dropped into oyster beds to target those animals whose pearls are ready. For that reason, they are sometimes known as *Pearl-Pursuing Missile Mussels*, but in fact the mechanism of their pearl collection is far more subtle. The pearl-seducing mussel emits a whistle, irresistible to the oyster, who immediately unlatches its shell to welcome the suitor. With a simple movement of its shell, the mussel creates an eddy of water that sucks up the pearl, and then it moves on to its next victim. This process has also given rise to the appellation *Swirl-Abusing Whistle Mussel*. Regardless of the name, the fisherman need only collect these pearl-packed mussels once their work is complete.

This remarkable increase in efficiency aside, we must also mention the services these new mussels perform when placed on dangerous reefs. With no oysters in the immediate vicinity, the *Whistle Mussels* pucker their lips—hypertrophied in this variety—and simply begin to whistle unrequitedly, in hopes of attracting their prey. Placed in sufficient number, this whistling is loud enough to be audible aboard a passing ship, thus notifying sailors of the peril lurking just some meters under the water, who can then shift course to avoid dashing their ships on the reef. Thus, the industrious *Pearl-Producing Mussel* will render the most useful services to humanity, while we can expect the *Pearl-Seducing Whistle Mussel* to replace the lighthouses and sirens currently in use in navigation.

Hunters nearly everywhere are showing interest in a new kind of bait offered in certain gunsmith's catalogs under the name *Pearls for Hares*.

The product is a little "imitation" pearl that one places in a clearing and which evokes the form, if not the color, characteristic of a rabbit's typical byproduct. The hare, astonished by these strange, lustrous droppings, stops, looks, sniffs, and at that moment it is completely vulnerable. At this point we must note that it is important not to confuse the *Pearl for Hares* with that produced by mussels, nor, in the unlikely event you ever cross one, with the product of *Pearl-Producing Muscles.* Jokers, whom I suspect lack chiseled physiques, have written to inquire if the *Whistle-Mussels* might not be of use on land, that is, as *Girl-Seducing Mussels.* Indeed! Though not because the female of our species is susceptible to the bivalve's crude mating call. The pearl-stealing eddies produced by the mussel underwater are transformed into a refreshing current of air on land. It makes a lovely gift for a lady, half pocket fan, half cooing companion animal. And, if crossbred with a *Pearl-Producing Mussel,* it will produce a *Girl-Seducing Pearls* for its master. (Men unable to afford this costly hybrid can always occasionally plant a *Pearl for Hares* between its lips.) Finally, let us add that it is important not to present the lady with the new *Snarl-Producing Mussel,* bred by oyster farmers to protect their beds by intimidating would-be predators, much like guard dogs. Similarly, farmers must avoid the *Pearl-Reducing Chisel Mussel,* a monstrosity of mussel husbandry whose bellicose behavior can decimate entire beds overnight. Obviously, a bit of caution will prevent any errors, but a simple "lapsus calami" when writing instructions could lead to regrettable mistakes.

Without shrinking from the administrative consequences of such an act, which are always unsettling, on the 15th of the preceding month, a citizen smashed the glass of a fire alarm located on the Quai Voltaire. An explosion had seemed to erupt between the chimneys of a building situated on the quai. When the firemen arrived, there was no trace of an explosion to be found. At most, it seemed, a few feathers were fluttering about in the air, and the courageous citizen was arrested, as one would expect.

After the same thing happened eighteen times in a row at the same location, it finally caught the attention of the fire chief, and after some hours of careful observation, he confirmed that they were observing *Avian Explosions.* How could such catastrophes, until then reserved for artificial birds, now be visiting these ancient little creatures? At first the matter appeared truly mysterious, but the director of the Municipal Laboratory was able to shed light on it.

To explain, we must expand this somewhat abstract commentary to include the curious evolution of Parisian sparrows, which, no longer able to find dung in the street, gradually began to subsist on the gasoline of automobiles. This diet, perfect in all other regards, has one grave fault. Under the influence of the animal's body heat, these essential oils release dangerous flammable vapors, and since sparrows have the adorable habit of building their nests next to chimneys, explosions could only be expected. And they occurred.

Immediately, the Society for the Protection of Animals began researching a new model of *Nest for Sparrows Made of Metal Screen.* Constructed a bit like a miner's lamp and produced by the thousands, these were placed on all the roofs of the capital. It is an onerous but inevitable consequence of progress.

In the big cities we are all too ignorant of the endless pains our horticulturists go through to produce the popular lettuce known as *Curly Endive.* A recent improvement has considerably reduced their difficult labor, but it will nonetheless certainly provoke the justified

GASTON DE PAWLOWSKI

ire of animal lovers everywhere. In our eastern regions, horticulturists have gotten the idea, it seems, to use domesticated storks, whose beaks' natural shape is perfectly fitted to the work required. One restrains the storks for some minutes while heating their beaks to a very high temperature over a series of gas lamps lit in advance. Then they're released into a field of endive. The poor beasts can think only of cooling down their glowing-hot beaks, and they descend upon the lettuce leaves for the contact with their vegetal moisture.

In less than ten minutes, it seems, ten well-prepared storks can curl an endive patch sixty meters long by one meter wide. Our horticulturists are overjoyed; but what can they possibly say to the concerns of the Society for the Protection of Animals?

The campaign undertaken by the Horse Lovers Society to eliminate blinders has had fortunate repercussions for our scientists' research. Without the blinders, it was noticed that some horses have defective vision, and solutions were immediately proposed, depending on the owner's wealth and the character of the horse—glasses, pince-nez, or even monocles. The scientists hastened to tell me that monocles only come into consideration for morning jaunts in the woods, glasses being easier to use in everyday Parisian traffic.

However, a recent announcement by the Academy of Medicine seems to render all these ideas irrelevant, along with the methods employed. It seems that a certain drug, based on atropine,[9] can modify the accommodation of the lens and naturally reduce or enlarge the size of objects (or at least the illusion of it) without any optical instrument.[10]

It's even said that this method has long been known among animal trainers and toreadors. Applying the drug a few minutes before a performance will cause a big cat to perceive the objects around it significantly enlarged. The poor lion thinks that it's a tiny thing compared to its twenty-meter-tall trainer; now it only wants to curl up in the palm of her hand. As for the bull, it humbly presents itself in the arena like a little morsel of beef at the bottom of an immense pot. This explains certain acts of bravura on the part of the trainers, which otherwise seem completely unjustified. We can also thank the Horse Lovers Society for revealing to us what lies behind certain safari hunts in Africa and India.

The *Ovidatum Poultry Marker* is an extremely interesting device placed behind laying hens, which allows their eggs to be imprinted by means of an ink roller at the moment of their production.

The fresh eggs thus come with a verified date stamp and a series number. With the *Ovidatum Poultry Marker* farmers can also tell the exact number of eggs laid by each hen. They can thus detect any foul play.

The device, sold with a little pair of suspenders, is compact, durable, and affordable. It's of interest to poultry farmers everywhere.

Our horticulturalists are delighted. The newly invented fruit bell hangs from the branches of apple and cherry trees. It makes a clear, silvery sound when a bird or other marauder alights on a branch of the tree, scaring them off.

Apple Bells and *Cherry Bells* are available depending on the tree, both painted and enameled to perfectly mimic the natural fruit.

Poultry farming is certainly all the rage, it seems, now that everyone has heard about a brilliant little device, which it is completely superfluous to describe, which forces chickens to lay *Square Eggs*. It offers great fiduciary advantages to packaging and shipping in large quantities. In many cases, breeders have even managed to produce hexagonal eggs, but that's just a question of degree, and the square egg is already on the right track.

For dog lovers, we'd like to present the new safety hinge now being mounted on the back of bulldogs' heads. During heat waves, the bulldog's mouth opens so wide that its jaws meet behind its neck and the skin of its head falls to the ground. With the security hinge, there's no longer anything to fear.

Since the spread of cubism, the use of the aforementioned *Poultry Ovirectilineator* has become widespread, allowing the easy packaging and shipment of square eggs. Unfortunately, this change has devastated our brave carnival entertainers, who can no longer procure ovoid eggs to shoot out of their water cannons. We are happy to recommend an easy substitute: the eggs of waterfowl, which fit nicely into cannons and, it seems, balance better on a jet of water.

The *Ambush* is a clever little artificial shrub that will delight our gardeners. It consists of a metal stem which allows the shrub to be planted in the ground, and it features elegantly shaped *coarse sandpaper leaves*. An attractive natural lettuce plant is placed at its peak. Slugs, which ravage gardens, try to reach the lettuce during the night and drag themselves onto the sheets of sandpaper. After hours of struggle, the skin of their abdomen becomes so thin that they develop peritonitis, and the slug dies, writhing on the sandpaper leaves of the *Ambush*. The gardener need only wash the shrub each morning and it's ready for reuse. We'd like to add that the *Ambush* is attractively designed. It will certainly be the prettiest ornament in the gardens of the outlying districts, where the flora is often a bit sparse.

Unfortunately, even the loveliest discoveries can be tarnished by misuse. The *Ambush* has not escaped this sad fate.

Some eccentrics—alas, one can never be free of them—got it in their heads to organize a slug race on a course four meters long made of sandpaper, endowed with significant prizes and christened the *Mucus Marathon*. The first slug to arrive at the goal, chest torn open, dying, receives a hefty prize, which is cynically pocketed by its owner. Doping, and particularly the use of tire sealant, is strictly prohibited.

This is a sick caprice, which shouldn't even earn a passing smile. It is a blight on horticulture and an egg on the face of zoology.

III

ADMINISTRATION — THE OFFICE — FINANCES — POLITICAL AND SOCIAL ECONOMY

Umbilical Monitoring — Finger-Nib Reservoir — Working Their Foreheads to the Bone — Floor Postings for Drunkards — The Storming of the Santé — Machine for Cutting Postage Stamp Perforations — Little S.W.A.K. Dogs — Administrative Errors — Greasy Election Posters — Transatlantic Telephones — Date-Stamping Wheels for Buses — Usage of Coins and Bills

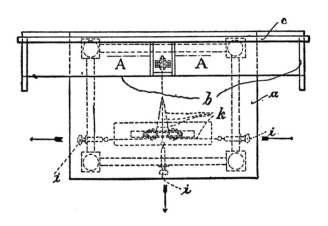

The Committee on Human Monitoring met for the first time this year at the Ministry of Justice. This very interesting project seeks to monitor all French people from the moment of their birth, as if they were gold or silver. A suitable numbering system would bring with it great simplifications in the establishment of public records, as well as individual taxation. As is known, the monitoring badge would be placed over the navel. This reform, which will perhaps provoke protest, would nonetheless be of interest in an orderly society at a moment when the state of our finances demands impeccable administrative organization.

How moving, how patriotic, one might say, regarding an initiative spontaneously undertaken by certain bureaucrats that is intended to reduce the French state's bloated budget by very modest means. The new *Finger Nibs* are currently being tested in our ministries. Instead of trimming or biting their nails for hours at a time, our bureaucrats have resolved to let them grow to a length of two or three centimeters. Then they'll trim them to obtain excellent pen nibs free of cost. The index finger will be shaped for everyday writing, while the thumb will be used for cursive script, and the pinkie will make a very serviceable drawing pen. The third and fourth fingers will be reserved for duplicate copies, which can be rendered at once on two overlapping sheets. The new *Finger Nibs* can also be modified to suit the needs of the individual. Generally, the less dexterous left hand should be reserved for tracing musical staffs in a single motion. Enthusiasm is running high in our ministries, and anything might come of our bureaucrats' noble spirit of competition. Undoubtedly there is already a *Finger-Nib Reservoir* to hold back the ink! There's also talk of hand tattoos that could be used in thousands of combinations for arithmetic calculations. Also under consideration: crossed-finger multiplication tables, a machine for calculating curvature for those with arthritic fingers, and a proportional compass for surveyors. But there's no need to be hasty; let's await the first results before delivering a definitive opinion. However, we will add that starting now, in the washbasins near the exits of the ministries, oxalic acid[11] will be available to any urbane functionary wishing to wash his nibs.

As far as the *Finger-Nib Reservoir* is concerned, I deny any personal responsibility over providing its description. Its execution would require nimble fingers; it couldn't be done by someone who was all thumbs.

To make a *Finger-Nib Reservoir*, the tip of the finger must be pressed for a second against a red-hot current-model stovepipe. If the operation is carried out correctly, a large liquid-filled blister will form. Then one need only insert a little drain of cotton soaked in aniline blue. The little drain is pressed against the trimmed nail, feeding the colored liquid down it throughout the day. Maintaining the *Finger-Nib Reservoir* is very simple after that, requiring only certain precautions at the outset. The interior of the blister must be sterilized with mercuric chloride,[12] then the little reservoir is tanned according to the method used to manufacture leather gloves. After a few days, when the blister is well established, it can be filled each morning like a fountain pen, by means of a simple ink syringe. It's a small thing, but it's a better distraction for our bureaucrats than producing weekly statements in triplicate stating the state of the state.

Whatever discoveries our economists might make on this subject, all too often we remain unaware of the horrors of working in the home. Did you know that in one poor district of a provincial town, the foreheads of elderly ladies were being used to crease skirts for our fashionistas, who had no idea of the odious labor taking place? It seems that the poor old ladies worked with prodigious speed, creasing their brows. A complaint has been filed against their exploiters.

They revealed the sad details of the procedure: the skirt is laid upon a table; the old lady, exhausted, rests her head on it, thinks of her troubles, and creases her brow. The movement is analogous to that made by a sewing machine. But we won't fixate on these cruel and purely technical details.

Here is a felicitous reform, which will please our civil servants, and which is a handy complement to the measures taken against alcoholism: from now on, signs warning against public drunkenness will be placed on the very floor of cabarets and no longer on the walls, at an inaccessible height.

Thus, a drunkard rolling about under the table can easily take note of them and meditate upon them at length. Hanging them near the ceiling is only of use to the healthy, a spot that, starting recently, is reserved for military notices and traffic ordinances.

Several years ago, in official milieus, the strange project of the Rive Gauche Committee for Democratic Festivities was discussed in veiled terms.

To fittingly celebrate the anniversary of the storming of the Bastille, this committee decided to organize, down to the last detail, the *Storming of the Santé Prison*.[13] Heated discourse was planned for a public park in Paris, then from there the demonstrators would head to the prison and open its doors, releasing prisoners indiscriminately, massacring the guards and tearing down the walls.

What makes this story all the more curious is that the organizers were animated by the best of patriotic intentions and that they believed they were doing good. It was all the police commissioner could do to make them understand that their project ran counter to public order and that it wasn't possible to generate contemporary unrest as a successful analogy to historic events, the prisoners of course being entirely different people.

Thus, the *Storming of the Santé* was replaced by a public ball, and this little affair, which could well have turned tragic, had the best of all possible outcomes.

It seems that before the year is out, *New Machines for Dividing Postage Stamp Perforations*, currently being manufactured by the civil service, will go into operation. We're wrong to lose faith in the civil service, as we all too often do; it's true that its reforms are slow, but ultimately common sense always prevails with them.

Everyone knows that large numbers of postage stamps are sold together in a single sheet. Originally, nothing separated the stamps, and the consumer had to cut them apart with scissors before using them. Long ago, the postal service thought to facilitate this process by separating each stamp from its neighbors by a little row of perforations. That already represented a major step forward! Today, this reform will be pursued to its logical conclusion. The perforation itself will be divided, and the stamps, freed from each other, can be used immediately for postage without any preparation.

The *New Machine for Dividing Postage Stamp Perforations* is a true miracle of precision. It's actually very difficult to separate each of the thin strands of paper connecting one stamp to those around it; it requires a highly advanced tracking system. It seems that its development is nearing completion, and we can soon expect the *Individual Stamp*, which the postal service has been working toward for over fifty years.

Another invention, inspiring and amusing in a different fashion, will be introduced at the same time in all French post offices. A *Little S.W.A.K. Dog* will be tied at each station to lick the stamps that patrons would like to attach to their letters. Training these little dogs is no small matter! It's a strange story: it seems the trainers got the idea to show the dogs stamps from Newfoundland, which depict the province's dog.

At this sight, the *Little S.W.A.K. Dogs* were all too eager to lick the back of the stamp, tears in their eyes. Now that they were in the habit, the *Little S.W.A.K. Dogs* continued their work without noticing that they were now licking our usual stamps depicting a woman sowing seed.

This felicitous innovation, which will be warmly welcomed by taxpayers, will be subject to strict regulation. Authorities fear that postal workers may abuse the new invention, so use of the *Little S.W.A.K. Dogs* will be exclusively reserved for stamps affixed by members of the public. Every evening when the office closes, the *Little S.W.A.K. Dogs* will be submerged in warm water for a few minutes to remove any accumulated adhesive. Once dried, they can perform a valuable service as guard dogs at night.

There was talk of complaints from the Society for the Protection of Animals, but that's one rumor we're able to refute; the little bureaucrats will be on the budget starting at the end of the year.

The minister of finance has just appointed a commission to investigate a new *High-Draft Anathermic Chimney*, which is predicted to provide great benefits at our major ministries. It's well known that, ever since regulations demanded that hearths be lit even if temperatures remained high, the employees at our ministries have suffered greatly from heat, and their work has been markedly impeded. The new *High-Draft Anathermic Chimney* completely absorbs all the heat emitted. In the offices where it is situated, it generates a temperature precisely equal to that outside. It's an invention we can't recommend strongly enough to all our civil services, which are forced to exhaust their budget lighting great fires when the heat waves haven't yet passed.

The government has covertly acquired exclusive rights to the use of a certain invention for the next elections, causing a great stir in political milieus. It's a patented model of an electoral poster on waterproof gummed paper, its surface completely coated in a thick layer of oil. Once posted, it's impossible to cover these posters with other posters; the paste simply slides off the oily surface, and competing posters slip pathetically to the bottom of the wall.

Though it's a bit of a straw-man argument, does the government really have the right to defend this sort of monopoly, if indirectly, on the part of the official candidates? An inquiry, it seems, is imminent.

It seems that for some time now, the Bureau of Communications has been planning for the establishment of new submarine telephone lines. Construction had already commenced when the Fishery Bureau countered with its veto. And do you know why? You'll never guess. Our telephones still often make a disagreeable *crackling* noise, which may frighten fish because it will remind them of the sound of frying. You can imagine the arguments extrapolated along these lines: the ruin of our fishing industry, and so on.

If the report issued today hadn't been an official one, such childishness would hardly be believed possible.

It is with pleasure that we present *Date-Stamping Wheels* for new Parisian buses and taxis, which will become mandatory in a few weeks. The tires of these wheels are made of juxtaposed pieces of rubber, analogous to those formerly used for bus wheels. These pieces will be shaped like the rubber date stamps used in our ministries. In the center, the date will be composed of mobile rubber figures, which would be changed each day. Only the vehicle number would always remain the same. An ink roller would always be in contact with the wheel.

With this new system, there will be no more delays, no more interminable violations at every intersection, no more tiresome conflicts with crowds. If a pedestrian is run over, he or she will automatically be stamped with the date of the accident and the vehicle number. Without interrupting the flow of traffic, the victim could be immediately transported to the hospital for the necessary treatment, while at the same time recording *on his or her person* all the information necessary for the investigation.

It's a truly substantial simplification, which our bureaucracy can justifiably wield with pride.

We would also like to suggest that for automobiles belonging to individuals, should this measure someday be applied to them, it would be nice to add some polite turn of phrase to the stamp, like those found on calling cards: "With my sincerest apologies," "My regrets," or "With condolences." That would give some small satisfaction to the victim, and it's a mark of tact and good upbringing on the part of the motorist.

The Ministry of Finance is bustling with work on a vast project to transform our currency, which will be better adapted to modern needs, taking a utilitarian form worthy of a great democracy. Copper and nickel coins will now be tapered on one side like a screwdriver, allowing mechanics—numerous as they are in our era—to always have the tool that is most useful to them in their pocket, while the center of the coin will be pierced with a hole that can be used to rethread worn screws.

Fifty-cent and ten-franc coins will have four holes, allowing them to be used as buttons on clothing or undergarments. Forty-sous coins can be used as an opisimeter, for measuring distances on maps.[14]

We would also like to highlight an interesting project to replace the old motto encircling five-franc coins with letters of the alphabet and Arabic numerals for quick and easy printing; the 100-sous coin could be a marvelous little *Pocket Typewriter* itself.

Then there are also the banknotes which feature geographic maps of our beautiful colonies, as well as advertisements for the most important products manufactured in France. Everyone will find something to like about this interesting transformation, which we are persuaded will be very well received.

IV

DIET — CUISINE — FRAUD

The Mucus Cruet — Telephone Fraud — Rabbit Licorice — Inedible
Oysters — The New Heavy Sparrows — The Salad Shaker Strike —
Shirts for Gruyère — New York Auto Butchers — Railroad Gardens
— The Seaphone — Cartridges with Juniper Berries — The Coffee Mill
Door — The Skewer Rifle — The Touring-Club Dog — Dairy Cars That
Prevent Milk from Turning

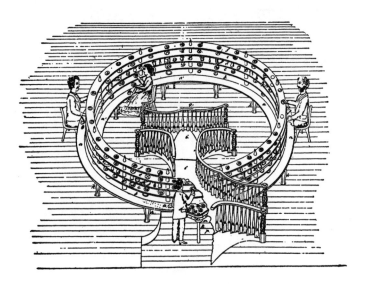

The *Mucus Cruet* is a new Kraut invention that will soon be greasing the wheels of success at many a small Berlin restaurant. It will be adopted by bourgeois Austrogoth families and will be found on all modest tables of central Europe.

As its name indicates, it consists of a slug that is fed a special diet of greasy kitchen waste. Rather than leaving a trail that is useless, sticky, and soon dry, it leaves an oily deposit, capable of seasoning a sizable salad in just a few minutes. Far from being an object of disgust when found in a salad bowl, its inventor claims, it will be welcomed by all of those on an average budget. Thanks to it, costly oil expenditures can be eliminated. One must only remember to remove this excellent household helper before eating the salad, so that it doesn't needlessly risk its precious life at the hands of clients or guests.

Attempts are currently underway to breed and domesticate a slug which naturally secretes vinegar, to be christened the *Acetic Mucus Cruet*. Up to this point, the attempts have been satisfactory but, let's say, unconvincing.

Food inspectors recently made a strange discovery. For some time now, they've been observing French-fry street vendors whom they believed were simply selling their customers old pieces of cardboard cleverly cut and soaked in oil. But then how to explain the delicious frying noise that attracts passersby and spurs them to buy this awful product? Nothing could be simpler. Most vendors are unscrupulous, and so they connect to the telephone system and conceal the device under their kettle, where the crackling noise—so unpleasant for telephone users—attracts pedestrians tormented by hunger. This is a new trend in telephone fraud, which our police couldn't have anticipated.

It seems the ingenuity of our swindlers knows no bounds, much to our chagrin. After some time, food inspectors were notified about the inexpensive boxes of licorice sold in great quantities in all the little grocery shops of the outlying districts.

The candies contained in these boxes are suspiciously reminiscent—I'll put it plainly—of rabbit droppings, and yet an analysis revealed that this curious product does contain licorice, albeit in very small proportions.

A meticulous investigation revealed that in those parts of Australia ravaged by rabbits, someone got the idea to plant hectare upon hectare of licorice bushes. As they dig their burrows, the rabbits eat the licorice roots, which is how this dubious product came to be sold to us today.

The Australians may be overjoyed, but it's up to our sanitary services to protect us.

We've gotten word that an investigation is underway into an all-night restaurant that, at celebrations, would serve oysters rendered chemically insoluble and doused in seawater to which a small amount of laxative had been added. It seems that oysters thus prepared can be served over and over again indefinitely. But we'll wait for the results of the investigation before speaking any further on this delicate subject, which demonstrates just how far certain scientific applications can be pushed in our era's hospitality industry.

A new invention always provokes a social or economic crisis, soon followed by development. Thus, at first the stagecoach industry was ruined by the invention of locomotives. Then, little by little, the stagecoach drivers became stationmasters, and the horses were put to work maneuvering the merchandise cars or feeding the guests at train-station cafés. After a few years of adjustment, order is restored and all that remains is progress.

We spoke earlier of the sad situation of Parisian sparrows since the disappearance of equine labor, which provided them with their daily bread. Saddened by the terrible state of things, the main taxi associations have decided to mix some grain in with their automobile oil to provide more or less suitable nourishment for the Parisian sparrows. Evidently, this was a last resort. And yet this simple last resort has provoked a veritable revolution in our diet. After a few months, the Parisian sparrows had gotten used to feeding on the oil and grease left on the ground by our automobiles. These lovely little winged creatures grew to tremendous proportions, and everywhere we went people pointed out the *New Heavy Sparrows* to us. These little fowl are now in high demand at our great restaurants. A little oily, no doubt a bit too greasy, their taste is strangely reminiscent of certain fish-eating birds. The gasoline may give them a strong bouquet, it's true, but it's not unpleasant, reminding gourmets of a certain waterfowl.

Just when we thought our poor little sparrows would disappear for lack of manure, we're confronted with a new breed of eating sparrow that can replace fowl on even the best of tables, in an era when hunting is restricted. It's just one of the thousand surprises with which progress delights us. It shows us that we should never despair of the future of humanity, and the few sparrow explosions spoken of earlier shouldn't diminish the importance of this little event.

Although it's perhaps more relevant to the local news or the domain of sociology, we would nonetheless like to point out the amusing solution presented by the *Salad Shaker Strike* at Swiss hotels. The British and American devotees of these palaces were called upon to use their cosmopolitan talents to aid the overwhelmed maître d's. Instead of shaking hands, everyone simply shook the salads, which made an excellent first impression all around.

Why, the inventions of our humorists hardly compare to the sensational discoveries science makes each day!

It's been announced that the great hosiery firms have received a sizable order for several thousand *Flannel Shirts for Gruyère*. They prevent potentially dangerous chills from overtaking the cheese when it starts to perspire.

It must be said, the shirts are of a special design. They're soon to be found in all good dairies.

As unlikely as it seems, a journal of diet and hygiene has alerted us to the opening in certain very poor New York neighborhoods of *New Auto Butchers*, similar to our old horse butchers, but evidently of a very inferior grade. Since most of the hansom cab horses have disappeared, finding food in the poorer quarters has become very difficult, and a clever industrialist has gotten it into his head to carve up old out-of-service automobile taxis for butchery.

It seems that the old leather from the carriage, soaked with grease, makes for a good enough stew, and that old tire casings macerated in gearshift oil are a fair imitation of duck. The treads, it's said, are very much like duck skin. Old valves are a very elegant substitute for the neck, and a few ball bearings swimming in grease give the impression of peas.

The old inner tubes also make very presentable tripe, once they've been patched, chopped, and macerated in a dilution. As for eel ragout, we're told that the ignition wires are a perfect replacement. And it's not just the old rolls of Chatterton and Cambouis that make agreeable sausages.[15]

Let us also add that the oil pans of old vehicles often contain runover dogs, chickens, or rats. Everything mixes in the oil, along with pins and nuts, making for an excellent lark pâté, which the poor devils on Long Island are very fond of. Isn't that a striking example of the ingenuity that is ever active in the Americans?

It's been astonishing, the number of notices posted in train cars, inviting travelers—in a rather insistent fashion—to make use of the water closets during the whole duration of the journey except during stops at train stations. We now have an explanation for this little mystery.

Its empathy aroused by the constantly rising cost of living, together with the great train lines, the government has begun a study of a series of measures which could soon revolutionize food production. Thousands of kilometers of arid soil along our train lines will be opened to agriculture. Depending on the nature of the terrain, either asparagus or cabbage will be planted there.

One first attempt at planting cabbage between the rails will be attempted on the Clermont-Ferrand line, and the project is already known familiarly among rail employees as the *Chew-Chew Train*.

The cabbage planted and cared for by the rail employees and level-crossing keepers will be watered by a special train, the *Veggie Express*, which will pull great containers of water. As you may have guessed, fertilizer will be provided by passenger trains.

When it comes time for the harvest, the *Veggie Express* will be composed of a scythe engine and several produce cars, which will simply whoosh down the line; cabbages cut by the special scythe at the front will be sent flying, thanks to the tremendous force and specially inclined planes, into the produce cars. Harvesting will thus be accomplished in just a few minutes and the train sent directly to the market halls once it arrives in Paris. This will prodigiously and rapidly revitalize the capital.

Charmed by this invention, an English company by the name of Way de fer Fisch has now proposed that a pit be dug between the rails of the level portion of the Calais-Paris line and filled with water. All edible sorts of fish will be acclimatized to this pit, and the catch will be brought in with a special train armed with a net, exactly like the Veggie Express.

It's a change that would certainly have its costs, but which could really spice up the food business.

The *Seaphone for Oysters* has been adopted this winter by all the big restaurants. It was used for the first time at a Christmas celebration.

It's a very simple little device, extremely ingenious, and similar to a phonograph, except that it perfectly recreates the sound of the sea. When they hear it, the oysters open themselves, thinking that they're under water. One must merely wedge them open with a little piece of wood so that they can't reclose, then serve them without further preparation. The restaurant staff needn't waste any more time shucking oysters, effortlessly satisfying the clientele.

Since it's still the season, we'd like to tell hunters about the new cartridges filled not with buckshot, but with juniper berries, for hunting thrushes. We know that juniper-fed thrushes cost more than plain ones. An ordinary thrush killed in this way has the same qualities as a thrush fed on juniper, a considerable advantage to the hunter.

We must draw your attention to the *New Coffee Mill Door*, laudable as much for its simplicity as for its practical ingenuity. Ultimately, it is a simple improvement on the revolving doors currently in use, which up to now had been intended to prevent drafts. The axis of the revolving door is prolonged into the basement of the cafe, and it connects to the establishment's usual coffee mill by means of gears. As the clients arrive, they push the revolving door. The coffee is automatically ground in the basement, and it doesn't take much thought to realize that the amount of coffee ground corresponds precisely to the number of visitors.

At dinner, a simple lever allows the coffee mill to be disengaged in order to connect the door to the mayonnaise. No more fretting, no more useless shouting, no more threats bellowed at the chef. The latter will find the precise amount of coffee or mayonnaise he needs without the least effort. When the clients leave, the gears connect the device to the vacuum cleaner to tidy up the carpets. This is a very practical invention, very American in spirit, which will soon be present at all our café-restaurants.

In the hunting world, there's been much talk of a new *Skewer Rifle* which will work wonders. We're not exaggerating. The idea is an old one: the bullet is replaced by a rotisserie skewer and the entire apparatus resembles the cable cannons familiar to the sailors among us. And what do our housewives think of birds that are skewered before being plucked and cleaned? The Skewer Rifle will only be accepted among the unrefined.

It's true that the inventor has also proposed a *Hollow Cylindrical Bullet Shaped Like an Apple Corer* for gourmets, which could be shot through the body of the bird beforehand. But this assumes exceptional aim on the part of the hunter, and to us the invention seems stuck in the realm of pure fantasy.

The new *Touring-Club Dog* for country inns so widely discussed of late is nothing more than a vulgar police dog trained in a certain fashion. As is well known, at small inns the *Touring-Club Dog* is tasked with filling in during personnel shortages. It cleans plates with its tongue, which, to be honest, is easy enough to achieve; then it dries and dusts them with its tail. This last task doesn't so much require training as it does a trick. One need only make the dog sit with its back turned to the plates and show it a piece of sugar. Immediately, the dog will wag its tail and the plates will be dried. They are available immediately to customers.

For dairymen, we'd like to highlight the new milk car with mobile body, which turns on bogies and allows the front of the car to be turned toward the back once the delivery boy has completed his route. This measure, which will be appreciated by technicians, was introduced to keep the milk from turning.

V

ARMAMENTS — MARINE DEFENSE — WARTIME STRATAGEMS

Duck di Guerra — Biplane Pigeons — French Boomerang — Bird Compass — Optimistic Binoculars — Self-Greasing Caterpillar Cartridge — Parrot Drill Sergeant — Artillery Shell with Nine-Hundred Kilometer Range — Airplane Trap — Planet Shells — Suicidal Electromagnet — Electric Oyster — Paste for Drivers — Bean-Powered Torpedo Boat — Aerial Cigar-Cutter — His Master's Voice — Sausages for the Attachment of Machine Guns — Rotating Heels for Krauts

Fig. 1

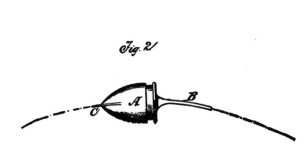

Fig. 2

Despite all precautions taken by our neighbors and future allies*
the Italians to carefully conceal their curious invention, everyone
has begun to talk covertly of the new *Duck di Guerra*, which they've
sent en masse to combat the Turks in Tripolitan North Africa. This
invention is certainly the most surprising and most characteristic
of our modern times. After the flight of birds inspired man to
develop aviation, inventors have now been inspired by recent innovations in aviation to transform birds into dangerous and useful
auxiliary support. The *Duck of War*—always female—is a wild and
robust species, which, over the course of several weeks, is adroitly
nourished with saltpeter, buckshot, glycerin, and potassium chlo-
rate. The voracious duck gladly adapts to this diet, which must be
administered in careful doses by skilled chemists. The duck of war
is then expedited to the field of battle in small cages that prevent
all movement and released in the direction of the enemy. The duck,
or, to make the matter clearer, *hen* of war flies over the army during
combat. Its all-too-comprehensible horror at the sight causes it to
expel the eggs loaded within it before its departure. Need I say that
these eggs are terrible explosives thanks to its prior diet? As they
fall to the ground, they wreak the most frightful devastation among
the ranks of the enemy, just like a bomb dropped from an airplane.

---

* I see no need to alter the prophetic terms of this note written some years before the war.

It has been calculated that a squadron of hens of war, released at the correct moment, could annihilate seven hundred hostile cavalrymen in thirty-five seconds. The secret to this curious invention lies completely in the dosage of its food. It will soon be discovered by everyone interested in aviatory or avian militarism. Let us add in closing that if, by chance, the mixture doesn't explode, the enemy army will forever remember the humiliation of having eggs of dubious quality dropped on their heads.

More now than ever, people are talking about *Military Biplane Pigeons*. It's been confirmed that recent trials have been made at the military dovecote in Satory. It's even been said that mysterious strangers have been seen roaming about recently in the countryside around Versailles.

Evidently, constant progress in aviation has had repercussions in the bird world, quite naturally leading to the idea of perfecting the flight of carrier pigeons by applying recent aeronautical discoveries to them. It's undeniable that for long voyages often undertaken in unsatisfactory meteorological conditions, the *Biplane Pigeon* offers more stability than the ordinary model *Monoplane Pigeon*. They're more difficult to flip and put up more resistance to the wind.

How are these new *Biplane Pigeons* made? Why, obviously from two pigeons superimposed upon one another, one of which possibly controls the steering. All suppositions on this point are well and good, but it's certain that up to now the secret has been well kept by military authorities. Some reporters have recently thought to question inhabitants in the area who are said to have seen the *New Biplane Pigeons*, but, no doubt fearing they might

GASTON DE PAWLOWSKI

betray military secrets, their responses have been limited to snickering, sometimes while battering the unfortunate journalists with incomprehensible jeers.

All their confused explanations boiled down to: "*It's like that every spring, one must really be from Paris to see things where nothing is there.*" Certain among them even rudely offered to show their biplane ducks, chickens, and dogs to some reporters sent from a big journal. What should we make of all of this? Let's hope that we'll soon have the key to this tiresome and interminable mystery.

One rather curious invention that was just presented at the institute is the new *French Boomerang,* whose wood is cut in such a way that once the instrument has been launched at the enemy *it does not return to the thrower*. He thus avoids all risk of injury.

The *Bird Compass* is a very simple, modest invention intended to revolutionize the aerial transport of telegrams, rendering inestimable service in times of war as a result.

The *Bird Compass* consists of a special little compass placed on a bird's head, a bit like a military cap, held on by means of a tiny chinstrap. This compass is unusual in that the needle pointing north is shaped like a V. This V is mobile and, like a caliper, it can open to a wider or narrower angle. Only one of the legs of the V is magnetized to point north. The other branch curls around and ends in a point that can poke the bird's cheek as it flies if it departs from the direction that it is intended to follow. I can't tell you how frequently this simple invention has rectified the flight of carrier pigeons, instantly putting these intelligent animals back on the right course. What's even better, placing this little hat on the head of the first bird to come along—be it a duck, a turkey, or even a sparrow—will transform it into a carrier pigeon capable of rendering useful services.

Depending on the destination of the pigeon, the angle of the calipers is set before departure, and the poking arm is placed to the right or left of the head, depending on the orientation in relation to the pole.

Nothing could be simpler; it can be put to use by all branches of the military based on topographical maps.

It's a little-known fact that the Kaiser has distributed field binoculars to his officers which contain stereoscopic views of Paris and Moscow imprinted on their lenses. The hope is to overstimulate the troops by giving them a glimpse of the success that is soon to come. This tactic had only mediocre results, and now we know the reason why: owing to the movements of the troops, a regrettable error occurred, in that binoculars with a view of the Eiffel Tower were given to soldiers leaving for the Russian front, while those with prospects of the Kremlin brought amusement to the banks of the Yser.

One really does wonder where the progress will end, which is made year after year to ensure the comfort of our young soldiers. Most recently, on the order of the Ministry of War, the pyrotechnic services have distributed new self-greasing *Caterpillar Cartridges* to all the barracks, destined to ensure practical and automatic lubrication of the weapon. The *Caterpillar Cartridge* is composed of a simple, ordinary Lebel rifle cartridge case containing an eight-millimeter caterpillar—fuzz not included—held in place by a clever Vaseline putty. Simply insert the cartridge in the rifle in the evening when placing it in the gun rack; in the morning, you'll find the barrel thoroughly greased. During the night, the caterpillar slowly climbs out of the cartridge and up the barrel, distributing the necessary Vaseline along its walls. To encourage and, if necessary, instigate its climb, one must simply adorn the upper part of the gun rack with some mulberry leaves, which can be mixed with laurels to preserve the military atmosphere. This may be the one innovation that will make our Ministry of War popular throughout the barracks.

Among all the latest sensational inventions, one must reserve a particular place for the anticipated introduction of *Parrot Drill Sergeants in the Army*. Contrary to recent rumors, the intention is neither to disrupt the high command, nor even to reorganize the current leadership.

The intention is only to fatigue the corporals and sergeants as little as possible with the elementary instruction of young recruits by substituting parrots responsible for communicating the habitual commands. It had been proposed to simply use phonographs, but phonographs lack vivacity and imagination in this area. Perhaps they will be imposed upon the Kraut army, but they will never have a place in our country. In times such as these, one wants to accustom young soldiers to obeying the most unexpected commands to whatever degree possible, in order to prepare them for real combat in the field. Parade exercises for marching in rank are of little use. What is expected of the French soldier is the unexpected, initiative, even imagination, and the parrot, whatever the professional critiques against it may be, could provide excellent results in this regard.

But you will see that this idea, excellent in principle, will not fail to provoke interminable objections, and that foreign armies will seize upon it long before we think to implement it in France.

The *Krautman Zeitung*, official organ of the "Diptheria Gesellschaft," provides curious details on the new artillery shell 980 currently being constructed in the factories of the Krupp firm, which can be launched nine hundred kilometers, perhaps longer. Owing to its dimensions, the shell cannot be shot from a cannon. Instead, it will be expedited by railway and contains six frozen meals for its warden.

A recent intelligence scandal has revealed curious and unexpected hidden sides of the prewar period.

We were stupefied to discover that Germany had laid *Airplane Traps* exactly like those constructed to trap birds. The bait consists of a few French flags draped on the ground over the trap.

At the same time, court proceedings have revealed to us that the French military aviation leadership had prepared similar traps, for their part, composed of a few clocks placed on the ground.

The practice has since been uncovered. What will they think of next!

Another great disappointment for the Krupp factories. Their recently developed cannon with a range of one hundred kilometers performed disastrously in trials. The initial speed of the shell was excellent; at 1,133 meters the shell overcame gravity, and the projectile was launched into space, never to return.

"When I create worlds, I for one don't work in clay like the Ancients; my planets are made of iron!" the Kaiser was heard to have said in an excess of lyricism which much concerned his entourage.

We have learned, through an indiscretion in an Austro-Hungarian military journal, the *Ostrovassalygoth Zeitung*, that the Krauts, desperate for innovation, established a colossal electromagnet in Flanders at the beginning of the war which, in case of an Allied attack, would pull rifles and machine guns toward it. They didn't count on our artillery shells, which, drawn from their original course by the electromagnet, obliterated the infernal machine, which exists no more.

Our greatest shipping companies are about to adopt the *new Electric Oyster for the detection of leaks*, which is destined to provide the greatest advantages. The oyster, alive and closed, is placed at the bottom of the hold at the beginning of the voyage. It is equipped with an electrical contact which activates an alarm as soon as the oyster begins to open.

If, by chance, water should penetrate the hold, the oyster quickly opens, the alarm is activated, and the captain can take immediate safety measures, gaining control over the gravity of the situation. In this way, we hope to avoid shipwrecks in the future.

The *Berlingoth Blatt*, voice of German motoring enthusiasts, advises drivers to coat their clothing with paste before departing on a journey. After a few hours on a dusty road, the motorist will become invisible, his uniform being precisely the color of the terrain. As for the driver's cap, dusted as it will be with gravel, it makes an excellent emery cloth of immediate use for all mechanical purposes.

The activities which the Kraut admiralty keep shrouded in the greatest mystery continue along the Kiel Canal. If our information is correct, it seems that they are testing a new *Torpedo Boat* called the *Bean Turbine*, capable of reaching the highest speeds, an accomplishment requiring a veritable revolution in the art of seafaring. All that is currently known is that the vessel's hold is filled with beans capable of producing a considerable volume of gas. How is this gas utilized? Via a simple combustion engine causing air to escape from the rear of the boat, turning a turbine? We can't be sure quite yet, but it seems to us that it will be difficult to hold in the secret for long. In any case, it seems to entail the elimination of coal for these light little ships, from which one expects great speed.

A marvelous new invention: the *Cigar-Cutter Airplane* for pursuing zeppelins.

Confident, victorious words were pronounced in German trenches after the Battle of the Yser. Three thousand phonographs sent from Berlin were responsible for that. In certain parts of Belgium, cinematographic projections were also arranged with silhouettes of fresh troops. General opinion in Germany is that these mechanical means will be sufficient to raise morale in the army.

To eliminate the embarrassing impression created throughout Europe by the discovery of German soldiers chained to their machine guns, the German General Staff has ordered new chains forged to look like a series of connected cylinders. That way the machine guns will appear to be attached to them by a string of sausages.

It has also been reported that twenty-seven machine-gun officers have been decorated, receiving iron collars with spikes.

Soon the entire German infantry will be equipped with rotating heels to facilitate maneuvers on both fronts.

Did you know that it's forbidden to use the German language aboard Kraut submarines? All those fricatives rapidly deplete the air supply on board.

To ward off a possible coal shortage, a very ingenious model of the new *Whaleboat Squadrons* has been introduced to the English Royal Navy. Already there's talk of equipping similar French squadrons for postal services. The new whaleboat simply consists of a current-model whale with a little waterproof chamber attached to its back by means of a girth strap, similar to a howdah on the back of an elephant, containing a postman and urgent dispatches. To steer the whale during its rapid journey across the ocean, they've dreamed up a device whose simplicity is at once marvelous and truly disconcerting. The postman is equipped with a long fishing pole with an *old whalebone corset* hanging at its end. When he wants to turn left, he simply hangs the corset in front of the whale's right eye. It flees to the left in terror, and vice versa. When he wants to go in a straight line, he must merely place the corset above and a little behind the head of this intelligent animal. To entertain himself on the long voyages across the Atlantic, the postman can also place hollow eggs on his faithful steed's blowhole and shoot them off with his rifle. All of this is extremely strange and perhaps a bit old-fashioned, it's true, but at the same time its modern elegance is truly delightful.

GASTON DE PAWLOWSKI

VI

RAILROADS —

URBAN AND MARITIME TRANSPORT

The Linocalcium — Mooing Train Cars and Apis Lamps for Cattle — Ice Tunnels — Musical Telegraph — Métro Incense Burner — Using Emigrants to Combat Tempests — Deluxe Telescoping Train — High-Speed Superheated Broth Trains — Automatic Ship Navigation — Panthéon-Courcelles — The Local Cyclemotive — Gummed Privacy Patches — Gut Rests for Train Cars

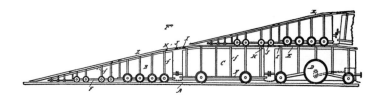

The *Linocalcium* is a new product that looks exactly like the linoleum that the state railway company has just adopted as flooring in its cars. It is made of calcium carbide chipboard backed with durable canvas.

We know how futile all the notices have been enjoining travelers not to spit on the floor of the cars. With *Linocalcium*, all of that will change: now the notices inform the travelers that, should they happen to spit on the ground, the carpet will immediately emit an intolerable garlicky odor. The travelers, concerned for their own comfort, will avoid spitting on the floor. It may be the first time that notices from the Committee for Hygiene have been so respected.

The first test showed no result, for the simple reason that these were carried out on the Southern Railway. This is an instructive and piquant detail in the anecdotal history of contemporary science.

Certain advertisers may have been too hasty when announcing the implementation of *Vestibulized Cattle Cars* throughout the state rail network to the press. You've doubtlessly read about the developments on this subject which have been published everywhere. From now on, just like in passenger cars, thanks to interconnected vestibules, the poor animals can move from one car to the next, visiting their friends, and so on. There's even talk of *Manger Cars* where the cattle can eat at certain hours, hygienic amenities, and heaven knows what else. That, it's said, is a bunch of bull. The truth is much simpler, but truly moving.

The state rail company has decided to place a sort of *Accordion* between each cattle car resembling a communication bellows. During the journey, the accordions will emit a mooing just like that of the cattle. With the abrupt starts of freight trains, the jolts produced by the cars while maneuvering, the flexing on curves, it will be a veritable orchestra of mooing during the voyage.

Why all this bellowing, you ask? It's simple—and this is why it is exceedingly touching: to console the unfortunate cattle, torn from the meadows of their birth and driven to the terrible, insatiable maws of the big cities. The cow, enchanted, believes that it hears its mother's voice. It falls silent and listens.

That's not all; the artificial mooing puts ideas about suckling into the poor voyagers' heads which can never be satisfied, and after a moment of joy at hearing their mother's voice, they're sadder than ever during the long journey. That's why the ceiling of the cattle cars has been adorned with lamps like those found in passenger cars, but equipped with glass teats which hang down from the globe. A milk reservoir placed in the ceiling of the wagon feeds the lamp, called the Apis lantern. Naturally, the cattle's attention is drawn to this luminous udder hanging from the ceiling. They raise their heads and console themselves by suckling on the long trip, firm in their belief in the maternal mooing provided by the accordions.

Soon human passengers will envy the amenities of cattle cars.

But frankly, it wasn't just love of animals that inspired this reform, but rather the desire that they arrive in good shape. The cattle, now silent, don't arrive fatigued the way they used to. They no longer arrive short of breath and barely able to stand. It's both a great benefit for the farmers and a consolation for those poor tender souls.

Taking advantage of the great cold, next winter the Paris Metropolitan Railway Company is going to carry out a project it has been researching for a long time: the digging of a tunnel through the ice under the Seine. Engineers will artificially lower temperatures by pumping in liquid air, aided by already low external temperatures. They then plan to freeze the water of the Seine and thus easily cut a tunnel through the ice within a few days. No more tanks of compressed air, no more onerous toil. They need only insert the metal tube containing the tracks and then they're ready for the thaw; the hermetically sealed tunnel will remain underwater. It's a marvelous expedient of modern science that all builders will admire. They've been thinking of using it to dig a tunnel under the English Channel, freezing the Strait of Dover for several months.

Since we're on the subject of the strange improvements that are currently being made to the railway network, we'd like to point out a charming invention that—alas!—isn't French. It's just been introduced on Spanish tracks: musical notation for the telegraph, in which little black disks are hung like notes from the telegraph wires. These notes play popular Spanish songs and travelers can sing along on their journey, reading the music noted on the wires. This innovation is all the rage in Spain. It can only be regarded favorably by a largely musical public which enjoys indulging in reverie. Entire scores will be thus depicted on long journeys, with medleys carefully orchestrated at junctions. On the return trip, the traveler can read the music in reverse, thus experiencing the most brilliant pieces of modern music. Keep in mind that the telegraph posts are indispensable for marking the measures, and that this notation is above all intended to enliven the leisure hours of passengers on commuter trains. On high-speed trains, it would require an astonishing virtuosity to sight-read the notation.

The administration of the Metropolitan has hit upon a truly elegant idea. At the station exits, the bins where one now throws away tickets will be replaced with *Incense Burners*. The tickets will be printed on Papier d'Arménie, which will spread a delicious odor throughout the ground floor when cast upon the burner.[16] The costs are minimal, and the results are excellent.

A little-known detail which I'm persuaded will be of interest to all of those who regularly travel our Transatlantic Ocean lines: do you know why a great number of emigrants from the south always embark upon our great luxury ships in sixth class, at very reduced prices? And do you also know why throughout the journey, they are fed dishes copiously seasoned with oil, as is the custom in Italy? With a little reflection, you'll soon understand what's afoot. In stormy weather, the emigrants, who have absorbed several liters of oil throughout the day, become ill from all the rocking, and I need not describe what happens in such cases. All the portholes are open, and the unwell emigrants stick their heads out of the vessel. Within minutes, the surface of the sea is covered in oil, and the tempest is calmed as if by magic. It would be silly to carry cumbersome barrels of oil, only to throw them in the sea in the case of a storm, where they'd be lost. With this method, the extrusion of the oil occurs automatically. It occurs only in case of great storms, when it is indispensable for calming the raging elements. It's a simple procedure, which costs little and ensures a peaceful voyage for first-class passengers, and passage nearly free of cost for the emigrants. This is the reason why one finds so many people from the Mediterranean among the sixth-class passengers, because the shipping lines prefer them, owing to their special ability to consume oily cuisine.

Starting next year on the line between Paris and Dijon, a new *Deluxe Telescoping Train* will go into service, the most wonderful and admirable improvement ever made to luxury trains in their history. We can now announce that *while maintaining the prudent velocity* of the current luxury train, which leaves Paris at 8:05 p.m. and arrives in Dijon just after midnight, *one could travel to Dijon in two hours eight minutes.* This might seem paradoxical. But its explanation is the most natural thing in the world once you've understood the formidable discovery recently made by an extremely modest and humble employee of the PLM Railway.

The idea is to take old corridor coaches emptied of their partitions and benches and turn them into one enormous flatbed train with the rear facing Paris while the engine faces Laroche.[17] The top of this immense, 155-kilometer-long train will form a jointed track on which a smaller luxury train with limited seating can travel at an equal speed. If the end of this gigantic train normally departs from the platform at 8:05 from Paris, the deluxe train will depart from the end of the gigantic train at the same time, traveling rapidly toward the front. Five minutes before reaching Dijon, when passing Plombières (Côte-d'Or), the deluxe train will have reached the front of the platform train, which will enter the Dijon station five minutes later, while its end will hardly have passed Laroche. Without changing the speed of the train, which up to now has taken three hours fifty-nine minutes to reach Dijon, the same destination will be reached in two hours eight minutes, which is all that customers can ask for. Safety, reasonable velocity, vertiginous speed—the new superimposed trains offer all of this. They may be a bit prohibitive in terms of material required, but they'll be highly attractive to busy people who will do anything to arrive on time.

They're also considering extending this deluxe train to Marseilles. After arriving in Dijon, it would simply have to pass to a platform train with its engine already at Mâcon, which would be perfectly level with the previous one. Thus, one could soon travel from Paris to Marseille *without increasing the velocity of the train* in seven hours at most, counting necessary delays for boarding and disembarking.

Next winter, the Eastern Company will put the new *High-Speed Superheated Broth Trains* into service, which will allow for extremely long voyages without changing locomotives. It's long been known that meat broth has the unique property of conserving heat almost indefinitely, but until now no one has thought of putting it to use for powering locomotives. Throw a few pieces of beef in the boiler, preheat it for a few hours, and hardly any coal will be needed to produce steam for the whole journey. Let us also add that, thus seasoned, the locomotive's water makes excellent soup, and that at any point during the journey, the passengers can serve themselves a comforting bowl of consommé by inserting ten cents into a faucet dispenser specially installed in each car. This invention will be especially popular in northern regions and will be implemented shortly on the Trans-Siberian. The latter would be transformed into a mixed freight and passenger train, carrying with it some spare cattle.

A navy officer recently asked me for some details on the *New Automatic Compass Ship Navigation* invented in America. It's best to clear matters up.

Many of our colleagues have written that the axis of the compass is equipped with a strong spring, which presses on the vessel, putting it back on course through the force of the magnetized needle. That's absurd. A magnetized needle, no matter how large, has never been able to push a ship back on course. Rather, the magnetized needle sends an electrical signal to the rudder. The ship is thus automatically set to rights by the compass. Officers on board can sleep soundly through the night without worry.

The public at large knows far too little of the desperate efforts made by the General Omnibus Company before it decided to discontinue service on the last horse-drawn lines from Panthéon to Courcelles and Wagram to Bastille. Countless ideas to improve the use of animal power were proposed by skillful technicians.

When they pretended to want to use the fermentation of potato peels to power the cars, or the rhythmic force of the horses' tongues, that was just a simple hoax. Utter nonsense. But there was a very serious project that the Company management decided on long ago, and whose economic appeal was very simple.

Taking advantage of cold winter weather, they planned to drive a wedge under the rear wheels of the omnibus. Then they would wait patiently for the arrival of spring. Of course, the sun beating on the sheet metal walls all day would dilate the vehicle, which, propped in the rear, would push the horses ahead a few millimeters. Then one need only wait for a cold snap, or even just nightfall, when the omnibus would contract and roll toward the horses, which, naturally have no reason to move. Each time more millimeters would be gained. Successive dilations and contractions could shift the omnibus appreciably. Obviously, this isn't the quickest of methods, but the commercial speed attained would in any case be notably superior to that achieved by dint of the company's horses alone.

But that's all history today; the autobus has put an end to these problems!

The *Local Cyclemotive* is an extra-light train in which passengers are seated not on benches but on bicycle seats. Equipped with pedals and chains, the passengers themselves propel the car, which can travel the rails at speeds far exceeding those of the little local trains.

These cars have been implemented on small secondary lines, so poorly serviced, especially during the summer season. Once a certain number of passengers arrive, a special car is immediately placed at their disposition.

Sportsmen on holiday and countryfolk returning from market can thus leave immediately, and should delays occur en route, they have no one to blame but themselves.

Passengers traveling in this way take up a quarter of the space, so the company saves on transport cost, and you can guess how welcome this innovation will be. If the test is successful, as we have every reason to believe it will be, it's been proposed that next year on the main lines, *Pleasure Trains* will be created, driven only by manpower, which will transport our Parisians to the sea for a ridiculously low price while also assuring them healthy exercise worthy of the highest praise.

As the holidays approach, we must draw your attention to the new *Gummed Privacy Patches*, which are sold in a little pocket-sized box. These *Gummed Privacy Patches* resemble wafers of sealing wax and imitate in full color the pustules caused by contagious diseases such as measles or scarlet fever. Before entering the car, stick a dozen on your face to ensure peace and quiet during a long journey. Even in the fullest of trains, this little trick will let you have your own compartment for the whole journey. The *Gummed Privacy Patches* can be easily removed using a moist sponge. They're in better taste than the stink bombs, epileptic soap, and fake rabid dogs currently in use.

Since obesity is always more widespread among the wealthy classes, our great rail lines have installed *Gut Rests* in first class cars, which will complement the armrests already to be found in the compartments. For ladies' compartments, extremely elegant bust supports are planned.

Thus, the irritating effects of a jostling train ride can be mitigated for the obese.

VII

FASHION — STYLE — CLOTHING —
EXTRAVAGANT NOVELTIES

Secret Dual-Fastening Dress — Adjustable Stovepipe Hat — Glass
Skating Rink for Flies — Wigs for Dogs — Diplomatic Pooch Pouch
— Personal Rear-View Mirror — Magnetic Handkerchiefs — The
Byzantine Ring — Shoe Funnel for Students — Artificial Felt — Prick
Pockets — Closed Signs — Muffler for Ladies — Viperine Gorgon Hat —
Living Birds for Hats — Pigeons for Racing Hats — The Westinghouse
Dogcar — Shoes with Drainage — Shark Boots — Water-Insulated
Thermal Garment — Storage Kangaroo — Mechanical Sweeping Skirt
for Elderly Overweight Women — The *Found It!* Collar Stud

It is with pleasure that we present the *Secret Dual-Fastening Dress for Socialites*, launched by a major Parisian couturier exclusively for his clientele. This new dress closes up the back like most other dresses, but it also possesses a second set of clasps on its side, completely hidden under a tiny piece of braided trim.

This dress is intended to give complete satisfactions to certain suspicious husbands who like to button their wife's dress themselves in the morning and unbutton it themselves at night to be certain that nothing about their artful personal fastening style has been modified. Thanks to its second series of clasps, the new dress means that nothing about this arrangement must change, and everyone is satisfied. It's an innocent subterfuge, similar to the dual ignition system so appreciated by motorists, which will be welcomed far and wide. We are convinced that it will contribute to the harmony of most Parisian households this season.

One of London's doyennes of elegance has written to alert me of a new trend among English club men this year. It's the *Adjustable Stovepipe Hat*. It is constructed just like an ordinary stovepipe hat, but it features an adjustment knob. The knob is placed on the side, allowing the wearer to aerate the inside of his tall hat at will by simply turning the knob. This will allow those fashionable men to not disturb this rather bulky headgear, and to be comfortable even in the hottest of weather.

We would also like to introduce the *New Glass Derby Hat Skating Rink for Flies* advocated for summer by the Society for the Protection of Animals. As we know, flies enjoy engaging in the innocent diversion of skating on well-polished heads. They're forced to abandon their exercise when the presence of a hat causes the rink to go dark. With the *New Glass Hat*, the flies can continue to skate as if in a real hall.

Hardly anyone wears wigs anymore, and our fashionistas are so sad that they won't be able to use all the countless frills and trimmings they bought last year. A new trend will improve their sorry situation. A few weeks ago in Le Bois, conclusive tests were carried out on *Wigs for Dogs* with extremely positive results. We've seen pugs with truly surprising manes and greyhounds delightfully coiffed in the style of Louis XIII. It's a trend that's certain to catch on this year, and which is certainly more logical than wigs for ladies.

While we're on the topic of dogs, we would like to recommend the new *Dog Cozy* made of wickerwork, which is shaped just like a suitcase with the bottom removed.

This *Cozy* allows dogs to be brought along free of charge without attracting the attention of railway employees. A chest strap keeps the device attached to the dog. The suitcase walks by itself; simply take it by the handle to give the appearance of carrying a suitcase (all while guiding the dog).

It's practical and handy.

In fashionable milieus, everyone is raving about the new *Little Rear-View Mirror* which milliners attach to large hats. It allows the wearer to see people following behind them, just as automobile chauffeurs can see cars to the rear thanks to the same little mirror. It's clever, stylish, and allows the wearer to maintain a dignified bearing while gathering indispensable information.

Also in the domain of fashion, and even more graceful and delicate, a major garment company is advertising the new *Handkerchief with Steel-Wool Monogram* for overweight people. This handkerchief is sold in a box along with a magnetized umbrella, which is indispensable for its use. Ladies whose girth has begun to expand fear abrupt movements which might breach the integrity of their corsets. Having lost faith in the gallantry of the younger generation, they fully appreciate the utility of such a device, which allows them to pick up their handkerchief, should it fall to the ground, with the magnetized end of the umbrella without having to bend over in the least.

The *New Byzantine Ring* for beggars will be very much in vogue this year. It looks like an ordinary ring, except for the fact that instead of being placed on top of the hand, the stone is affixed to the palm side. Thus, it is seen more often.

The *New Shoe Funnel for Students* with flared sides makes it easy to pick up bills and coins that slip through the many holes in one's trouser pockets. It's very economical for families. The device is simple. It consists of a brass wire which encircles the open end of the sock, holding it up with a support clipped onto the shoe.

The low prices charged by vacuum cleaning companies lately are astonishing. For just a few francs, you can have your entire house cleaned today!

A scientific journal has offered us the key to this mystery. The dust gathered from the carpet is sprayed onto paper forms for bowler hats, which are covered with a durable glue. In this way, a hatter can instantly produce a magnificent felt model in the perfect color, which can be sold to the public without raising an eyebrow.

We've just gotten word from London's Strand about a great tailor who has introduced a trend which will be all the rage this winter. It's the new *Prick Pockets*, which already appear on all elegant winter overcoats.

The interior of each pocket is lined with two little leather patches covered in rows of fine needles which point downward. When a hand is inserted into such a pocket, it feels a smooth sensation, like stroking silk. But upon removal, the needles sink deep into the flesh, and the tactless person cannot withdraw it. Thus, one can immediately thwart those indelicate gentlemen who don't hesitate to take a rewarding journey of exploration through other people's coat pockets.

Detectives are overjoyed, but we must note that the use of pockets modified in this way demands a bit of caution. At first you may inadvertently put your hands in your own pockets, and you'll have to return home without waving to anyone, a victim of your own trap. But that's just a matter of habit, and our amateur police officers are delighted at this new trend.

For this winter, we'd like to take note of a very strange, very Parisian fashion: that of dress shirts with the word "closed" printed on them in large type. The amusing part is that this trend is inspired by the signs which postal employees place at their counters when they want to be left alone. Many Parisians who are obligated to spend every evening at the theaters and restaurants always see the same people, but they often just want to have a quiet night out without seeming rude. Now they need only wear a sign saying CLOSED. Everyone understands. No one says a word to them, and they are exempted from all social niceties. It's a very intelligent trend, which reconciles the demands of society with the need for solitude which we all feel sometimes.

Here is a lovely creation that would make a tasteful holiday gift: the *Muffler for Ladies* in adhesive-lined pink silk stretches to fit perfectly around the mouth and can be purchased in an elegant gift box.

The muffler is similar to the sort used for automobiles. It prevents any yammering, discussion, or tiresome conversation, while still allowing the lady to say everything she wants. Absolute silence prevails, and that's the important thing. In winter, the muffler for ladies also prevents the flu and sore throats. It falls elegantly on the shoulder like a boa, and its sophistication will appeal to all women.

For the sake of documentary completeness, another variant exists: the *Boorishness Muffler for Men*. But we'll forgo discussion of these luxuries and matters of good taste in this collection dedicated entirely to science.

Despite its somewhat pretentious name, I believe that the *Viperine Gorgon Hat* is destined to be extremely useful to all meticulous travelers who hate it when a stranger suddenly sits on their hat in a train car or restaurant.

The *Viperine Gorgon Hat* is a derby hat of the usual model, topped with a spike, and which conceals a tiny phonographic device.

When some oaf tries to sit on the hat, he immediately receives a triple warning: first, the sharp little spike gives him a poke, posteriorly. Simultaneously, the little phonograph emits a distinct hissing and speaks the word "viper!"

These three simultaneous warnings have an immediate and instinctive effect on the oaf, who immediately leaps up, preventing him from crushing the innocent hat.

This little instrument is discreet and convenient, and it guarantees the safety of one's hat.

Moved by the well-founded outcry from the Society for the Protection of Animals regarding the bird massacre carried out each year by the fashion houses, for summer this year our fashionistas have started a new trend: the new *Straw Hat with Living Birds* will be all the rage at our seaside resorts. The bird (parrot or pheasant) is connected to the hat by an elegant little chain. It gracefully poses, positioning itself variably, giving the same hat a new look each day. It's a true money-saver for the family budget, and it's also uplifting since these little winged creatures are undoubtedly pampered with little treats and kindnesses.

There's also been talk of starting a new trend of *Racing Hats with Pigeons*. These intelligent animals, released at the last minute, can deliver the complete racing results to the man of the house who has remained at home alone to look after the children. The same pigeons can be sent separately by airplane, should the family be traveling or on holiday, and since they garnish our socialite's hats, they don't take up any trunk space.

The *Westinghouse Dogcar* is a wonderful little invention, and highly practical, which will delight elegant ladies who enjoy promenading. Toy dogs can be placed on this little board with wheels, which can be pulled by a leash, so that they don't have to walk in the mud. The little animal's two front paws, as well as its rear left paw, are affixed to the board with laces. Only the rear right foot is free to be lifted.

When the little dog lifts this paw, it shifts its weight to the front left paw, which rests on a pedal. This motion brakes the wheels forcefully, and the vehicle stops. The dog owner immediately senses resistance at the end of the leash. She stops, turns around, and gives her dog the moment's pause it requires.

It's clean, graceful, and sells for a very low price.

Speaking of inclement spring weather, many people complain about constantly having muddy feet, which causes them to catch all sorts of colds. It's well known that, little by little, shoes become permeated with water, and that this water, not knowing how to escape, remains inside the boot—at the wearer's peril.

Motivated by this problem, a popular bootmaker is selling a new shoe with a hole the size of a two-franc coin under its sole, which will allow water to immediately drain away once it has penetrated the shoe. It's one of the most intelligent innovations we've ever had the pleasure to present.

We will conclude by adding that military suppliers who have adopted this boot improved on the original by adding a simple cork.

GASTON DE PAWLOWSKI

Remove the cork to drain the water from the sole, then replace it to prevent more from entering. It's practical and inexpensive.

Now for a more down-to-earth idea: the new *Dentures for Gaping Shoes* have been enthusiastically adopted by most of our beggars operating on the main streets. It seems that the hostile appearance of these shoes frightens off any guard dog who dares approach the vagabond. This amusing invention is also eminently philanthropic, obviously.

The new American garment in thermal rubber is double walled. Fill it with hot water, and you have an overcoat that will protect you from severe winter weather. Empty, it takes up little space in a suitcase.

Here is a new trend from Australia. It's currently the talk of the town in New York, and we can only expect that it will soon be adopted by our elegant Parisiennes. It's the *Storage Kangaroo*, which, on a morning jaunt to Le Bois or while running errands around the city, takes the place of a little dog, which has now fallen out of fashion. The latter lacks the indispensable practicality which has made the kangaroo such a success today.

We know that current fashion prevents the use of pockets, and so women are obliged to carry a little bag filled with all the useless objects necessary to them. Thanks to the kangaroo, this cumbersome bag has become superfluous, and the happy proprietress of this familiar animal can simply store what she needs in the animal's natural pouch. To prevent these items from falling out en route, particularly given the kangaroo's jolting gait, its abdominal pouch is equipped with a snap button, attached by means of a simple operation that can be performed without difficulty, like piercing an ear. This button can be embellished with a diamond or ruby, and the kangaroo's natural pocket can be lined with silk or batiste.

There's a new fashion which has developed based on the Dung Tricycles mentioned above: *Mechanical Sweeping Skirts for Elderly Overweight Women*. Whereas other long skirts kick up a thick cloud of dust, the sweeping skirt features a rotating broom underneath, which whisks everything it encounters on the ground into an interior pocket. That explains the improved cleanliness of our sidewalks.

But the main advantage for these overweight elderly ladies is to gather the items they've dropped on the floor in this interior pocket without having to bend over. No more burst corsets, no more dangerous maneuvering which could cause a stroke. The elderly obese lady need only walk scornfully past the place where she dropped something, and the object will be automatically picked up by the rotating broom. It's simple, hygienic, and convenient.

Less practical and significant but of everyday interest is the new *Found It!* collar stud, which I believe will prove to be very useful.

If it falls to the ground, this collar stud points tip up, taking the form of a common nail with a flat head. To find it, one must only remove one's socks and walk along the area of carpet where the stud fell off. Within a few minutes, intense pain will reveal its location, and one need only pull it out of one's foot and put it back in place. Thus, one avoids long searches, which are always so irritating for businessmen who must quickly dress themselves in the morning.

VIII

THE HOME — FURNITURE —
CLEANING UTENSILS

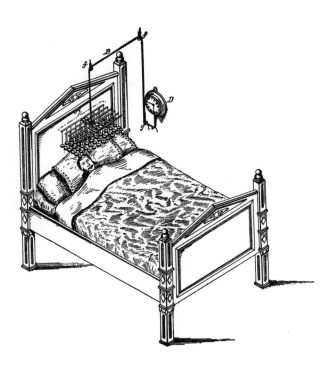

For the nouveau riche who own villas in the outlying districts, we present the new *Guard Dog Chains Made of Imitation Sausage*. These lightweight, painted aluminum chains are similar to those mentioned for Kraut machine gunners, but these are superior; they add an air of wealth to the property and cost even less.

One product we can't recommend enough: the new *Electromagnetic Walls and Ceilings* for cramped, squalid dwellings. This device, happily named the *Electrical Xavier de Maistre*, allows the resident—wearing shoes with iron soles—to walk around their room, on the walls as well as the ceiling.[18] This has a positive impact on the cleanliness of the apartment, since the resident can easily stomp on a spider walking across the ceiling.

Alas!—we must admit that the new *Phosphorescent Funnel-Shaped Keyhole* for drunkards is extremely useful. It allows them to enter their home without hesitation, even after copious libations. The *Phosphorescent Funnel Keyhole* can be found at all good locksmiths. It comes in two models: the regular one, and a reinforced model for delirium tremens.

The reinforced model is identical to the ordinary model; it differs only in that the hole around the lock is *magnetized*. The magnet can simply be used to guide the key toward the hole. But it can also be used in concert with a large electromagnet attached to the other side of the door, for the purpose of righting the drunkard holding the key in his hand, even if he starts to fall down the stairs. It's a practical, simple invention whose artistic execution is praiseworthy. Voluminous correspondence on this subject delivered to the Academy of Sciences each day shows how much interest this invention has generated among numerous bourgeois families. As such, I feel obligated to expound upon the slightest details.

In general, housewives are anxious to know *how, once the key has been inserted in the lock, one can be assured of the rotation of the drunkard*, allowing him to open the door. Nothing could be simpler. (Please understand I am writing for those with an earnest interest in the subject matter, and not for pranksters who see crude allusions in these serious technical reports.) It's very simple to ensure *the rotation of the drunkard*. Assume, for the sake of illustration, that the lock opens by turning the key to the right. One must first outfit the drunkard's right wrist with an elegant bracelet with the key hanging from it. As such, when the drunkard returns, he is forced to use his right hand to open the door. When the key is inserted into the lock, an electrical current flows, illuminating a little image of a large glass of cognac positioned to his right. Instinctively, the drunkard—very thirsty after climbing several flights of stairs—will want to grab the glass. Since only his left hand is free, he will move it rightward, over the other hand which is engaged in the lock. *This gesture will produce rotation*, and the door will open.

A locksmith from Argenteuil also wrote to ask how the drunkard can remove his key from the magnetized lock once the door has been opened. It's very easy: once the lock has been opened, the electrical current which drives the electromagnet stops, and the drunkard's own weight pulls the key from the lock. The description may be a bit complicated, but in practice, it's child's play.

Among the usual household items, we would like to make note of the new *Sieve with a Single Hole*. This exceedingly practical device allows a wide variety of highly resistant objects to pass through it. This sieve is composed of a handle with a simple metal hoop at one end.

For the summer season we'd like to highlight a new mosquito net which only measures five centimeters per side. Until now, a very small amount of space was left for the person sleeping under the mosquito net, abandoning the rest of the room to the little insects. It's more logical to place the mosquitoes in a small gauze box and reserve the bedroom for its human inhabitant. This modification will be met with joy in the Mediterranean countries.

The *Clockwork Chair* is a new armchair intended for meetings, which will be very useful for busy people who receive many visitors throughout the day. This armchair is placed in front of the desk of a minister or some other important person, and the supplicant is seated upon it. Once they are seated, their weight triggers the movement of a clockwork and the seat, mounted on a pivot, begins turning slowly. It completes a half revolution in five minutes. After two or three minutes of conversation, the intruder notices that they are seated in profile and are obliged to turn their head to continue talking. The irritation soon proves excessive, causing them to stand. The person of influence takes advantage of the situation by pretending to think that the visitor is leaving. If, by chance, one finds oneself in the presence of an incorrigible bore (after five minutes) who remains seated and talks while facing the wrong way, at that point it's easy to slip away. Five minutes later the supplicant will once again be facing the desk, only to discover that their interlocutor has left. It's a discreet and elegant system for ridding oneself of nuisances. It will be highly appreciated in all the big government offices.

The Academy of Medicine has informed me of an invention intended to revolutionize society—high society and low society, certain jokers might add. You always encounter them when you begin examining the most surprising discoveries regarding the human mind. It's the new *Pump Spring for Mattresses*.

It's hard to comprehend the vast amount of energy wasted in a big city like Paris each night by the countless back-and-forth motions made on mattresses. What could be cleverer and more useful than adding a little force and suction pump to each spring? The energy thus collected in a reservoir could be put to a thousand uses.

After a night of tossing and turning, a chauffeur or cyclist could open a simple valve to inflate his tires to the desired pressure. In other cases, the energy could be used to pump water into a basin if running water is not available.

GASTON DE PAWLOWSKI

Even simpler, the pump could drive a fan during heat waves, cooling agitated sleepers. In certain Parisian apartments, the force produced could be used to drive an elevator, allowing a late-coming, tipsy spouse to return home and set his wife at ease, after she'd been worrying in his absence, fidgeting in bed.

In all these cases, the production of energy is proportional to the needs, and calm will return on its own when the needs at hand are satisfied. It's a very simple little invention, highly practical, which will soon be found in all Parisian mattresses.

Among recent discoveries, we must make note of the remarkable use of the tides *for uncorking bottles*. At low tide, simply twist a corkscrew into a bottle and attach it by means of a cable to a ship moored at the harbor. As the tide rises, the cork will naturally be extracted—provided, of course, that the bottle is held firmly in place on the shore.

Isn't it funny to think that just a few years ago the Institute declared that the force of the tides could never be put to practical use?

Modern furnishings improve with each passing day. Lately they've come up with the new *Black and White Checkerboard Ceiling* for the bedroom. If beds are placed at each end of the room, the two occupants can effortlessly play checkers on the ceiling by means of little hand-held electrical lamps, which project the glowing round game pieces overhead. The glowing checkers are white for one opponent and red for the other to avoid any confusion. The game is played in complete tranquility lying on one's back, interrupted only when one party falls asleep and continued in case of mutual insomnia. It's a winning move for modern comfort.

For domestic servants working in large estates, we'd like to present the new suction cup for keyholes known as the *Louis XVI*, which proves useful in the world of well-mannered servants. The *Louis XVI* is a rubber suction cup with a magnifying glass at its center that is placed over keyholes. Elderly butlers, weakened by advancing age, need no longer place themselves in danger of contracting an ophthalmia due to the currents of air inevitably produced by keyholes. The magnifying glass also allows them to effortlessly see what's going on in the bedroom if their vision is weak. In all the best houses, the *Louis XVI* will soon be the elegant monocle preferred by all the domestics.

The new *Roller Sheets* are much more practical than an alarm clock. They also have the great advantage of being silent, so there's no risk of pointlessly waking the neighbors. The device consists of a sturdy spring controlled by a clockwork placed at the foot of the bed, which activates a wooden roller attached to the sheets. When it's time to get up, the clockworks pull the spring and the sheets instantly roll back, exposing the sleeper. They can moan all they like, making useless excuses; after a few minutes, they have to face reality.

People who use the *Roller Sheets* are strongly advised to sleep in a normal position, with their head near the headboard. Some accidents occurred during the testing period: a few sleepers got their feet caught in the gears and were rolled up with their sheets when the alarm went off. It's a regrettable accident, but easy enough to avoid if a few precautions are taken.

In our unsettled era, everyone will appreciate the new *Automobile Furniture*, which a big furnishings firm has announced. This furniture set can be linked together to form a train that moves of its own accord, rendering moving trucks superfluous. A kitchen stove provides the driving force—it can be transformed into a steam engine. Sideboards on wheels are attached behind it with very elegant chains, then rolling beds, sofas, and chairs, all of which feature very sturdy wheels. Moving house can be put on the fast track. The entire set travels full steam ahead in the street; the elements must merely be spread throughout the different rooms of the new apartment upon arrival.

Of all the little useful inventions hawked by peddlers for New Year's Day, we must point out the simple and ingenious new *Electric Doorbell*. Now, there's nothing new about electric doorbells, but this one functions on a different principle. To rid oneself of irritating guests, one must simply divert an electrical current from the lighting and cause it to flow through the button of this doorbell, which is made of metal. As soon as the creditors or undesirables have placed their hand on the buzzer, they're shocked to learn that their visit is unwanted. It's simple and inexpensive.

Recently, people have been asking for information on the new *Miniature Alarm-Clock Firecracker for Heavy Sleepers*, which has recently been released by a Kraut firm. This system, besides being brutal, is nothing new. The firecracker is placed in the sleeper's nostril at night and is lit at the appointed time by a simple lens which focuses the sun. One adjusts the time on a sundial connected to the firecracker by a safety fuse. At a set time, the firecracker explodes and, generally, the sleeper immediately awakens. It's a crude system, of use to brutes perhaps, but we can't recommend it for refined people.

We can, however, strongly recommend the new *Electric Piano for Novices*, a necessity today in all modern homes. This training piano contains only the keyboard; each note is electrically relayed to a separate piano case located in the cellar. A microphone helmet placed on the student's head allows them to hear the noise of the piano in the basement; the neighbors aren't inconvenienced, and thus the learner can pursue their studies day and night without interruption.

We hasten to add that there is no relation between this invention and the numerous cases of madness observed recently among coopers and workers charged with maintaining furnaces in cellars.

For all those housewives eager to make frugal use of their materials, the new *Rubber Tile for Kitchens* causes items to bounce without breaking.

Among all the novelties developed this season, we must point out the new *Hollow Soup Spoon* for children. Its handle is hollow, allowing the spoon to be turned in all directions without spilling a drop of soup on the tablecloth.

Certain people complain that when they go to bed, they have too much space above their heads and too little to stretch out their legs. We can recommend to them the new mattresses manufactured by a large firm, which are longer toward the foot end and shorter at the head. It's a very useful innovation, which must be adopted by all hotels.

For people uninterested in this invention who generally sleep curled up, the new *Round Beds* can be placed in the center of the room, pleasantly improving air circulation.

It's a true pleasure for me to announce a lovely, elegant little invention made by a pharmacist from the outlying districts: the *Wax Turpentine Biscuit for Toy Apartment Dogs*. Please excuse our perhaps excessive enthusiasm on this subject. All owners of small city dogs understand the felicitous results—or residues, we should say—to be expected from such food: no more stains on the carpets, which must be constantly replaced, no more irritating discussions with the concierge. Just give it a polish and in a few minutes the apartment and stairs will be shining like mirrors.

The *Redoutable* is a lovely gift to give children for the New Year.[19] It's a box of accessories that allow the child to transform a grand piano into a battleship in just a few minutes with the most marvelous results. A smokestack and two lattice masts are bolted onto the piano. A piston placed inside imitates the sound of the engine by striking the lowest strings. A bit brace allows the children to drill holes in the sides of the piano to accommodate the muzzles of cannons, as well as anchor chains. Electrical lighting can also be installed on the masts. This toy is sure to have great success with children, and will also develop military values in them, which any patriotic family must be pleased to instill in its offspring.

IX

AUTOMOBILES — AVIATION —

MOUNTAINEERING — HUNTING SPORT

Vag Project — Way Signs — Headlight Cinema for Police — Water in
Place of Gasoline — Magnifying Game Bag — Mont Eiffel — A 24/30
— Cricket Tennis Ball — Rigid Veil for Small Cars — Furnishings for
Alpine Summits — The Battle to Eliminate Nails on the Road — Rubber
Trees — Car Pedals for Pianos — Glowworms for Animal Illumination
— Racecar Body Vaccination — Little Kit for Repairing All Breakdowns

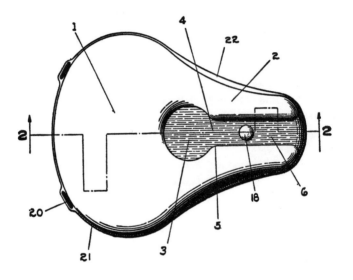

A certain Mr. Vag sent me a long statement concerning his eponymous project for *Aerial Navigation*. According to this inventor, it would be easy to write the names of cities in the blue of the sky by bleaching it with sulfur vapors. That way, pilots could easily find their way. A phosphorous mixture could illuminate the labels at night (though it would be dangerous in case of thunderstorms).

I briefly mention this project but have no time for its discussion. However, certain objections immediately come to mind. First of all, were we to inscribe such signs in the sky, what would prevent advertisers from making use of this new form of publicity? An unsightly jumble of advertisements and geographical notices would result. Wouldn't it be simpler to make the stars more useful by shifting them into more logical positions? As we know, the Pole star is located well above Poland, Leo isn't exactly above the city of Lion, nor is Orion above Villette.[20] Some shifts in location would be easy enough to realize by means of the telescope's curious ability to draw stars nearer or push them away.

It was with great surprise that certain motorists caught sight of signposts while leaving Paris that read *snozeb-enneragal*. It was simply a new signage method marking the direction of *La Garenne-Bezons*. This new system of notation will be extended to all routes. Given the ever-increasing speed of cars, it is more rational to write the signs in the direction of travel so that they can be read more quickly. This innovation has long been applied in England, particularly on the route to Newhaven. Our neighbors chose to name this town *Newhaven*-Harbour simply because it can nearly be read the same way in both directions.[21]

Still on the subject of way markers for motorists, we must mention that certain villages have posted highly amusing signs. When entering a town, one often encounters signs like this one: *Please slow down, the mayor is getting a bit old.* Then at the exit, one finds another sign with the simple words *Thank you!* Some speed-loving drivers have hung another sign after this last one: *Don't mention it!* If nothing else, these new signs have the merit of sincerity.

The *Headlight Cinema* is a new invention that will delight drivers and keep them from paying many fines. By means of a small mechanism attached by a belt to the fan, the vehicle's headlight can be turned into a cinema which projects images onto the ground.

The film for avoiding fines depicts a huge python writhing on the ground in front of the car. When the officers catch sight of this vehicle pursuing a terrible serpent convulsing desperately on the road, they flee in fear and don't dare to solicit a fine. It's a bit simple but it's something to be considered.

Let us add that different images can delight travelers on their excursions. Comical scenes can be projected onto walls at night in the country while a tire is being repaired; the canvas cover of a market truck could also be used while the driver is asleep, and one is forced to creep slowly behind this old farm cart for several kilometers.

As summer is approaching, numerous motorists have written to me in great excitement that one can *replace gasoline with water to drive an engine*. You see, it eliminates all chance of fire, and what economy! Drivers immediately understand the benefit—but how to do it?

The process is very simple. It was revealed to me on a recent excursion around Paris. While having lunch, one must simply ask a service boy at the restaurant to put water in the radiator. Nine times out of ten, experience tells us, when one gets up from the table and examines the automobile, the gas tank has been filled with water. The process, you see, costs little. As for the results in practice, it's even simpler: the car no longer works, but the method is now understood, and that's the important part.

For hunters, we recommend the new *Game Bag* whose cover consists of a magnifying glass. Thus, one can return home with little sparrows or tiny mice without being ridiculed by railway employees who will think you're returning with a hare or a partridge.

Starting next year, a large construction project will begin to transform the Eiffel Tower into the Matterhorn. For some time now, Parisian winters have faced regrettable competition from the sports practiced in Switzerland. The Eiffel Tower will be turned into an exact replica of the Matterhorn by means of reinforced concrete facades. Ascents of its faces will be organized, and mountaineers will experience all the sensations of vertigo and danger that they seek in the Alps. Its more gently sloping sides will be converted into toboggan runs. And the Parisian road system, such as it is today, will give mountaineers the chaotic impression of a mountain ramble.

This year automobiles will have a positive influence—can you believe it?—on French manners and social practices. Just as one designates the engine power with paired numbers *in horses*, ladies' ages are similarly designated in our salons. When speaking of a young girl of marriageable age, one would say: *That's an 18/24*; of a young woman: *That's a 24/30*. The designation 30/40 would be reserved for ladies who are still in the full flower of their beauty. Beyond these figures, one would employ simple and imaginative designations that are a bit more vague. One might say: *That's a spacious sedan, very comfortable for city driving*, or: *A lightweight racing car with a lot of power under the hood*. Of course, one would avoid offensive designations such as: *old jalopy* or *Paris to Amsterdam on fumes*. Certain expressions such as *double headlights* for married women, *smooth suspension*, and many others, could convey more intimate information, especially about women whose appeal may be particularly carnal.

A little invention which will be much sought after by our young people on holiday is the new *Tennis Ball Containing a Little Cage for a Cricket*. When the ball gets lost in tall grass, one need only listen to find it, making long, tiring searches unnecessary.

GASTON DE PAWLOWSKI

Let us recall that crickets can be attracted and captured by winding up a watch.

For owners of small, slow automobiles, we strongly recommend the new *Ladies' Hat with Rigid Veil,* which will be all the rage this summer. Whatever the actual speed of the vehicle, even in the complete absence of wind, the veil—supported by a little iron framework—will appear to be swept sidewards and behind the hat, giving spectators the illusion of great speed. This impression will be enough to preserve the self-esteem of the driver whose car never surpasses ten kilometers per hour.

Worried by numerous accidents this year, the French Alpine Club has established a commission for taking any necessary safety measures as soon as possible. After investigation, it was confirmed that most mountaineering accidents occur during ascent of the summits. Why? The reason is very simple: these stone summits are extremely primitive. They feature none of the comforts typically provided for industrial summits, for example—leather armchairs, mahogany tables, and the like.

One need only provide a modest level of comfort to reduce the likelihood of accident on a mountain summit. The Alpine Club started its work improving these conditions right away.

If table and chairs were provided, it would be very easy for the mountaineers to anchor themselves to these by means of rope. It's truly a pity that this indispensable improvement wasn't made earlier. But what can be said about the indifference of our mountaineers, who didn't even take note that the summits of our Alps were unfurnished, barbarically anchoring their ropes directly into the rock face?

The Touring Club of France has taken very practical measures for quickly getting rid of the nails found everywhere on the roads, which pose a danger to bicycle tires. Forty thousand magnetized horseshoes have been distributed to country folk for free. In addition, six hundred ostriches have been put into service on the promenades of the city of Paris. They're counting on these fascinating animals to eat and digest the nails found on our avenues, all while lending the main Parisian boulevards an undeniable mark of elegance.

The National Roads Bureau has finally been moved to action by the many automobile accidents caused by the presence of trees on the waysides of our road system. A car that would otherwise insert itself gracefully in the neighboring cabbage patch instead smashes against the rigid trunk of a sycamore; the fatal accidents caused in this way are innumerable. On the other hand, it would be difficult to deprive pedestrians of cool shade during the summer, which they need.

A very felicitous solution has been proposed, which, strangely, will earn a fortune for our great colonial ventures. The idea—if you haven't guessed it already—is to replace all the usual sycamore, chestnut, and locust trees with rubber trees, whose leaves provide equally good shade, and whose trunk gives way when struck violently with an automobile. The car, braked by the rubber trunk, will be pushed back by the tree's elastic characteristics and automatically placed back on the road.

Despite their respect for tradition, piano makers must concede to their clients' ever more persistent demands. Today, nearly everyone rides in automobiles, which results in irritating misunderstandings. When a driver is seated in front of a piano, if they play a wrong note, they instinctively depress the clutch pedal; that is, they press on the soft pedal, which is perfect, but sometimes in a very serious case, they want to brake abruptly, and they stomp vigorously on the damper pedal. To remedy this flaw, one must simply move the damper pedal to the right, to the position typically occupied by the accelerator. This is really an insignificant modification. It leads to greater success in practice.

We're pleased to announce the new *Glowworm Lanterns*, which, starting next year, will be hung on all animals who wander the roads at night.

We'd also like to highlight the curious tests a Parisian doctor has conducted on *The Vaccination of Racecar Bodies*, with excellent results. It's well known that car bodies are particularly vulnerable to the unpleasant consequences of smallpox, and that after a bout of it they nearly always are speckled all over with little holes for the rest of their lives; and we all know about the dangerous possibilities of a rupture. Vaccination eliminates this very real danger. In order to lighten the car, a racer can always hire a mechanic with smallpox scars specially for the track. This will lower the weight of the car without compromising stability at all.

A large firm on the Avenue de la Grande Armée that sells accessories for automobiles—to whom we owe the *Pump for Large Automobiles*, which connects directly to the driver's wallet, sparing them from operations which are intermediary, tiring, and useless—has invented a new *Little Repair Kit*, an improved replacement for the imposing equipment one has been obligated to carry in the trunk of cars until now.

This kit consists simply of an elegant, crushed-dog leather bag. It contains a little placard on which the following message is scrawled in large characters: *"I beg the officers not to write up a ticket if they find that I have left my vehicle until tonight. I've gone to Paris to seek help."*

With this simple repair kit, drivers no longer have any need to worry. Even if they are struck by the worst possible breakdown, understand nothing of the tangled wires around the battery, if each attempt to start the car is met with the abrupt recoil of the crank—they needn't care. Simply remove the sign from the bag and prop it delicately on the hood of the car. Then, move several meters away, and wait patiently behind a portico or a newsstand.

In a well-organized city such as Paris, it won't take ten minutes before skillful thieves approach the vehicle and read the inscription. Immediately, with remarkable aptitude and the sort of dexterity one hopes for vainly from the most capable mechanic-saboteurs found in a garage, they tickle the throttle, jiggle the levers, readjust the wires, and slide under the car, putting everything back in place.

When the purring of the engine convinces the driver that everything is back in shape, they need only come forth and reclaim natural possession of their car, which has been definitively repaired.

Depending on the driver's character, they might depart prudently, without consideration for the vexed thieves. Or, if they're soft-hearted, they might give the thieves the tip they've earned. It's a question of tact and sentiment.

X

CIVIL AND RELIGIOUS ARCHITECTURE

Ancient Temple Columns — Privately Produced Gas — House-Jack
Construction Site — Elevator Buildings — Rigid Plumb Line — Wings
for Villas — The Excelsior Phoenix — The Faubourg Montmartre
Altitude Cure — Musical Gates — The Water Scale — Broadway's Sky
Milkers

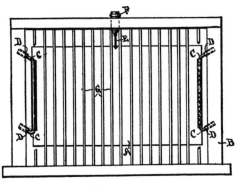

Fig.1.

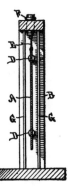

Fig.2

According to a report presented at the Academy of Berlin, it seems that the columns outside of ancient temples were simply scaffolding, intended to be removed once the monument was completed. See just how all the architectural conceptions we might have held regarding antique monuments are upended; soon archaeology will have demolished all our illusions. We will confine ourselves to noting that the scaffolding of yore had an allure completely foreign to our own!

In this volume, written for a refined public, our readers will understand if we don't dwell too long on the *New Cesspit-Fed Lean Gas Engine.*[22] It's a democratically minded invention, useful for expense-averse families and economical for industry, but which evidently lacks delicacy.

Mechanical cranes and metal scaffolding revolutionized the construction of our modern buildings some time ago.

All of that seems like child's play now that a new American construction system is being used for the first time in Paris, informally known as the *House-Jack Construction Site.*

The entire construction site is located in the cellar. One floor is constructed, then the house is lifted a few meters by means of hydraulic presses. Thus, one first sees the roof constructed at ground level, then the sixth story, then the fifth. That allows the upper floors to be rented easily and immediately, since they are pleasant to visit, being provisionally located on the ground floor or garden level.

The building rises little by little, and the construction in the basement doesn't bother the inhabitants at all.

Apropos this elevational system of construction, everyone in the architectural world is talking about the *New Elevator House*, which will soon be delivered by a big, fortified cement factory out of Long Island. The entire house, as it was developed by American engineers, is one enormous elevator, which can sink into the ground until it is level with the sidewalk. It would take far too long to enumerate the countless advantages presented by such a device: the elimination of interior stairs, or elevators in the case of skyscrapers; unlimited construction height, even in Paris and despite all the regulations in place, since it could sink to the necessary height should an Architectural Services inspector arrive.

To *bring up the post*, the concierge need only go out to the courtyard, press a button, and lower the desired floor to his level. Visitors standing outside can also control the building, which will descend before them to the story they wish to enter. No more useless steps, no more taking the elevator in vain. The first visitor to come along can simply call down the desired floor. The same goes

GASTON DE PAWLOWSKI

for repairs: painting the facade, roofing—all this work can be carried out without difficulty from the sidewalk.

Intelligent people will particularly appreciate this device, which allows them to rid themselves of a visitor by calmly pushing them onto the sidewalk and then rising skyward unencumbered.

Obviously, in this type of new building, shops would frequently be plunged into darkness, and certain building owners have objected to the diminished rents which might result. The pamphlet *The American Home* explains that this is all a regrettable misunderstanding. Electric lighting is sufficient to automatically ensure the desired amount of light, and as for the window displays disappearing below ground, this can only contribute to the movement of the wares. Clients hesitating outside on the sidewalk will hasten inside the shop to buy an object when they hear building-elevator's electric bell sound, and then they'll find themselves trapped in the store twenty meters below ground, and at that point it will be very difficult for them to leave without buying something. Several elevator buildings will be constructed in Paris on the new roads. It even seems that a great department store, thus renovated, plans to install a square on its roof which will be accessible to the public at ground level on Sundays. Here we have a happy solution to the agonizing question of open spaces in Paris.

All construction workers know how much time is wasted with the old plumb lines, made with flexible wire, which swing interminably before finally standing still. The new *Plumb Line with Rigid Rod* eliminates this irritating inconvenience.

This summer everyone is talking about *Mobile Wings with Feathers* for villas. These "building wings" replace the old tile or zinc roof. Thanks to an ingenious mechanism, the building flaps these wings in the morning to air itself out. They close at night to warm the inhabitants.

The general idea is charming, picturesque, and of an innocent simplicity suitable to a rustic habitation.

The details of our home design are truly inspiring. An architect recently informed me of a new device, which—despite its ambitious and rather ridiculous title—could prove very useful: the *Excelsior Phoenix*. In short, it is a little service elevator which takes bottles from the wine cellar one by one and brings them up to the living quarters, without needlessly fatiguing the personnel. It doesn't cost the owner anything to operate this elevator (and that's why it's earned its title of *Phoenix*). The *Excelsior* is controlled by a counterweight fed by wastewater from the washrooms and water closets. It functions with absolute regularity and perfectly in proportion, if I may say so, to one's needs. Nothing could be more clean, hygienic, or modern than this automatic device.

On this point, we would like to strongly contest the rumors spread by ill-wishing competitors after the first tests, when one feared the *reappearance* of the counterweight. A safety catch prevents the device from running backward, rendering distribution errors strictly impossible.

The Faubourg Montmartre and Himalayan Air-Cure Hotel-Sanatorium will be another of Paris's curiosities starting next year. The managers of this new palace have received authorization to permanently keep a gigantic balloon suspended three thousand two hundred meters above it. Breathing tubes suspended from the balloon will pour pure mountain air into the hotel. Mountain scenes will be painted on the courtyard walls. As for the rest, the illusion will be complete: as usual, bad weather will prevent travelers from going out on excursions, and from now on the vegetation of Faubourg Montmartre will be that found at two thousand meters altitude.

It's an innovation which will doubtlessly revolutionize the alpine hotel industry.

For the wealthy owners of villas, we'd like to point out the new *Organ-Pipe Gates*, which produce marvelous results from the slightest gust of wind.

Along with this model for castles, there is another for more modest dwellings. I'm referring to the *Countryside Kazoo Enclosure* with *Rustic Panpipes Gate*. It's elegant, amusing, and affordable.

People everywhere are complaining about the noise of flushing toilets audible in modern buildings made of reinforced concrete.

This noise is unproblematic in a grand mountain hotel: it would make the travelers think that they were still residing near that lovely waterfall generated by the turbines of the electrical plant. But in Paris, the problem is a different one: the noise can be heard on every floor, an irritating inconvenience. The Society of French Architects has definitively adopted a lovely flushing device that will eliminate this problem. It's the *water scale*. A little piano is mounted on top of the tank and is activated by the flowing water. Each time it is used, the device plays two or three scales, convincingly imitating the sound of a young girl having a piano lesson. This noise, common among bourgeois families, covers that of the flushing water. It evokes only artistic associations, immediately lending the building a general tone of distinction and wealth, which the noise of the toilet fails to provide. It's a trifle, I know, but it's by means of a million trifles which our bourgeoisie affirms each day anew its desire for elegance and taste.

The latest mail from New York brought us curious details about the new *Sky Milker* buildings they're building on Broadway. The *Sky Milkers*—which have already been vulgarly baptized *Vaches-à-ciel* in Paris—are one of Edison's brilliant innovations.

They receive their sustenance almost entirely from above; the sky fulfills these giant buildings' daily needs. Cleverly placed antennae allow the *Sky Milkers* to gather electricity from the clouds for illumination, and to power the mechanisms of the building.

Powerful suction devices draw water from the clouds for the inhabitants' daily use. Of course, the device also captures passing birds; it has an automatic sorting mechanism, which diverts the captured birds to be used in the building's kitchens. Heat, electricity, food, motion, washing, hygiene—the *Sky Milkers* provide for themselves, without recourse to urban supply companies.

The New Yorkers also hope that these new buildings will agreeably transform the climate of the entire country. All the clouds will be exhausted to provide for daily life, and the sky will always be as perfectly clear as that of Africa.

The creation of *Sky Milker* buildings is a fascinating embodiment of the idealistic aspirations of our friends in America.

XI

POLICE — COURTS —

PUBLIC THOROUGHFARES

Molded Fingerprints — Little Police Girls — Cerberines — A
Smugglers' Trick — Rubber Street Lamps — Taxi Palfreys — Magnetic
Posts — Rolling Sidewalks — Floating Officers — Little Waterfalls —
Camouflaged Dogs — Janus Chairs — Paoli Gyroscope — Peacock
Sweepers — Coal Trafficking — Wounded Actors for Pharmacists —
Glass Detective Eye

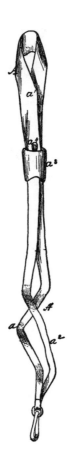

The police have just undertaken a very interesting raid in a Montmartre glove shop, and the following has become clear: the *Sticky Fingers* should have attracted their attention long ago.

The tale is rather strange. For the past several months the criminology laboratory has confirmed with bewilderment that most of the fingerprints taken from crime scenes—from the furniture and walls, after shocking murders—have been the well-known prints of police higher-ups, sometimes even those of the Police Commissioner himself or the General Prosecutor. This matter has baffled even our finest detectives. It was only in the course of the police search mentioned above that they discovered a stockpile of rubber gloves featuring the fingerprints of our Republic's most famous individuals. The gloves, sold to criminals, allowed them to accomplish their villainy without the least risk to themselves.

The new *Little Police Girls* will only be on patrol in early spring, in order to definitively rid the Bois de Boulogne of the foul lechers who disgrace it.

Perhaps it would have been better to keep this measure an absolute secret, especially from the press, because the satyrs themselves might read bits of newspapers left behind after Parisian families picnic in the grass on Sunday afternoons. But the indiscretion has already been committed and it's too late to hush it up.

Might one also condemn the choice of central brigade officers to play the role of the *Police Girls* in the Bois de Boulogne? Will it be so easy for these brave officers to conceal their height and black mustaches under a feminine disguise? Those in high places have assured us that considerable physical strength is needed to take the delinquents into custody.

We won't harp on the point . . . Besides, it's an extremely delicate subject, and any measures taken are good ones if they succeed, even if they adopt the *Booby-Trap Mannequins* they've spoken of.

An enthusiastic public recently crowded around the first *Cerberines* for dogs that they've started constructing on the boulevards. To simplify a bit, these little kiosks resemble the typical public urinals known as *Vespasiennes* and, like them, they've been christened with a classical name whose discretion won't offend.

These little structures have become completely indispensable after a short time. As we're all aware, a new regulation has gone into effect with high fines raised against dogs who have an accident on the sidewalk. The situation had become unbearable for them. We can only applaud this generous initiative undertaken by the municipal council, which demonstrates that it too knows how to be *good for the animals*, and which takes into consideration even our little friends' most piddling needs.

The truly unusual part of this new arrangement is the creation of a new brigade of *Privy Pups*, which provide the vital service of "priming the pump," so to speak, every morning at 5:00 a.m. in these little municipal facilities. It's well known that dogs lack initiative in such cases, preferring instead to follow the example of their confederates in the place indicated.

It seems the pernicious ingenuity of our smugglers knows no bounds. The problem arouses our justified concern. Today they have no compunction about employing the newest scientific advancement, endangering the lives of those who bravely serve the state to obtain what are ultimately mediocre financial gains. A recent investigation led under the utmost secrecy in a department in the east revealed shocking information on this subject.

For some time now the smugglers have been in the habit of firing several revolver, pistol, or rifle shots at the customs agents without trying to cross the border. Then they escape without making any profit. The unfortunate customs agents are immediately transported to a neighboring hospital whose name we will refrain from mentioning, where the bullets are removed. In general, the customs agents were only superficially wounded and were soon on their feet again. One similarity bound all these attacks: the strange disappearance of the bullets after their extraction. The police took notice, and reached the shocking conclusion that the hospital's low-level staff was committing acts of fraud. To make a long story short: the bullets were simply little balls of tobacco that crossed the border in disguise, evading all regulation. The scandal has inflamed the entire region. There's talk of arrests. We must add that the hospital's medical director energetically denies any complicity with the low-level staff.

The new *Reinforced Rubber Street Lamp* was tested with tremendous success before a commission of municipal councilors.

A bus driving at full speed can run over the gas lamp, which automatically bounces back to its original shape thanks to a coil spring, all without damaging its mica panes.

Alas—if only we could also construct reinforced rubber pedestrians!

Taxis had better behave themselves; horses are coming back. At least that's what we glean from the new *Taxi Palfrey*, launched recently in Paris by a group of breeders. The group keeps its *Taxi Palfreys* in an outlying district, and it was only by dint of an indiscreet inhabitant of Levallois that we became aware of this interesting development.

With the approval of the police prefecture, the *Taxi Palfrey Society* intends to allow six thousand riding horses to circulate freely in Paris. They are even-tempered, easygoing beasts who wear a taximeter saddle equipped with a little spike in the center, which retracts back into the seat when a twenty-sous piece is inserted into the meter. Thus, passersby can make use of the horse to complete urgent errands. Ten minutes later, a little alarm sounds, and the spike reemerges automatically from the saddle unless the rider inserts another twenty-cent coin to use the horse for ten more minutes.

It's a very economical system, which we don't doubt will become a major trend. Our fashionable men and women will love to go shopping and pay visits on horseback. A tip is out of the question, though a simple sugar cube may be a nice gesture. For its part, the company pockets all the profits and no longer has to fear a strike. The trained horses will park themselves along the curb when the rider leaves them, and instructions have been given to Paris customs officers not to let them wander beyond the barriers marking the city limits. As for the danger represented by the existence of Paris's countless restaurants, it won't pose a problem because the *Taxi Palfrey Society* will only employ used horses unsuitable for culinary applications.

The police prefecture is currently considering installing new *Magnetic Posts*, which will be placed at the busiest intersections of our most populous quarters, and whose external form will resemble those boxes for calling the fire station. The device contains a very powerful electromagnet capable of attracting any iron objects in its vicinity. In recent times, our hospital services have been overwhelmed, unable to provide enough surgeons to extract all the knives which find their way into the bodies of our pedestrians each day. These *Magnetic Posts* will make it unnecessary to disturb a doctor for these cases. The wounded party will simply be placed facing the electromagnet, or they may place themselves, should they wish to avoid the indiscretion of the police. The knife will be immediately extracted, and our housewives can also use the *magnetic posts* throughout the day to remove bits of needles or steel wool stuck in their fingers. It's a measure which the public welfare system has been demanding for some time, and which will provide considerable relief for our doctors.

The trade union of concierges and building managers is upset about a recent preliminary inquiry into whether the installation of moving walkways would be in the public interest on the sidewalks of Paris's busiest streets. How should they calmly accept the associated costs if, by sitting outside their doors in a state of contemplation, they run the risk of being swept several meters away? Our brave concierges have thought of a simple solution. They'll buy a chair with wheels to place on the sidewalk, attached to the doorknob with a length of strong rope. They could spend highly agreeable summer nights in this fashion, smoking their pipes without abandoning their watch over the building entrusted to them.

People crowded the banks of the Seine near Pont-Neuf to observe the courageous efforts of the new river brigade officers, recently recruited by our police chief. These new officers are tasked with aiding those who have thrown themselves into the river, or pedestrians who accidentally fall in and don't know how to swim, but the best part is *they've chosen officers with floating kidneys*. These officers are so adept at treading water that they will have no difficulty dragging people to the shore. It's a particularly shrewd initiative, and the enthusiasm of the crowd as it watched the agents brave the muddy water nearly reached a state of delirium.

Kraut industry is always encroaching upon our territories. The influential Germanic company located on the rapids of the Rhine which, as is well known, uses hydroelectric power wherever its metastases proliferate has purchased, by means of intermediaries, a concession for all of the waterfalls located in the Seine department.[23] It is believed that the influential company first had the idea to harness the power of all of the minuscule waterfalls produced in certain public facilities, working under the characteristic name of *French Society of French People for French Waterfalls*. Their force would power revolving advertising posters which would pass, one after the next, before the rapt eyes of the attentive spectator. It's a very German idea, which we can only consider with embarrassment.

During the most recent police target practice, it was shocking to observe that those much-lauded police dogs failed to participate. What people didn't notice was that a cowherd was stationed nearby, driving some little cows, along with a shepherd guiding some sheep with a tree branch. These little cows and sheep were none other than adroitly *camouflaged* police dogs under the direction of undercover officers. The police dog's profile is far too recognizable today, it seems, for these intelligent animals to be used in investigations. It was thus decided to tailor sheep or cow suits for them, and to apply makeup to ensure that the subterfuge goes unnoticed. In this way, a sheep can trot stupidly down a back road without looking suspicious, or a little cow can graze before a house under observation, and no one notices a thing. I need hardly add that these sheep don't fear the butcher, and that they enjoy taking on their natural role each evening when they return to the police station.

Beginning next month, *New Two-Faced Janus Chairs* will be put into service on our public walkways, eliminating the need for those women who rent out chairs. The rocking chair seat features elegant upholstery on one side and sharp spikes on the other. When ten cents are inserted into the back of the chair, it begins to rock and the upholstery side faces up, replacing the spikes. When the occupant gets up, the side with the spikes turns upward.

Many readers have asked me to describe the new *Paoli Gyroscope* in use in many police stations, whose first trial runs were kept a secret. It's simply a gyroscopic helmet that one affixes to a drunkard's head before taking him to the station. Thanks to the premounted gyroscope, the drunkard doesn't fall and can be peaceably driven to the lock-up, despite leaning precariously to the front, the rear, or to the side.

Yet another bit of old Paris is disappearing. After the street-sweeper vehicles and moving walkways mentioned above, now our municipal council, in the spirit of modernity and elegance, has purchased fifty beautiful peacocks who have been tasked with sweeping the gutters of the Champs-Elysées and the Avenue du Bois from now on. Just as the water begins to flow, the road laborers must simply toss down a kilo of fresh grain. Then they let the peacocks do their work. Attracted by the grain and following the current, the peacocks walk down the avenue with their feet in the water, picking at

GASTON DE PAWLOWSKI

grain here and there, while their tails, dragging to the left and right in the water, ensure a perfectly clean sweep.

Undoubtedly, many artists will cry out—how can you employ this magnificent bird, pride of Juno, for the basest needs of the city fathers?! What sacrilege! But ultimately, one must live in the spirit of the times, and frankly, we must recognize that the peacock sweepers' morning route down our avenues is suited to a city such as Paris. It's a highly preferable replacement for the daily sight of those brave people armed with brooms who were once charged with this difficult work.

For some time now we've beheld the astonishing sight, mainly in the mornings, of all the travelers from the outlying districts leaning out of the windows during their journey, attentively looking in the direction of the locomotive's travel. Do they fear an accident? Do they simply want some fresh air? This same motion interested all the rail employees intensely. We've just discovered the key to this mystery. The Criminal Investigative Bureau recently arrested thirty-five travelers on a worker's train at the Saint-Lazare Train Station just as they were showing their tickets; all of them were carrying a piece of coal lodged in their eyes. All these travelers have made a full confession. Fearing a rise in the price of coal, they wanted to stock up for themselves as rapidly as possible, to the detriment of our great railway companies. They will be prosecuted, as you might expect, because the company wants to make an example of them.

Each day the pharmacy business gets worse and worse owing to excessive competition. How to attract customers to such-and-such pharmacy? No one is interested in tapeworms anymore, and no other worms have proven profitable.

Clever pharmacists have discovered an amusing procedure for attracting crowds to their shops. During the day, they pay someone to pretend to be wounded, who is carried into the shop with their face smeared in red. A crowd immediately enters the pharmacy to see the wounded person, and since they have to buy something to justify their presence, the pharmacy attains considerable profits in just a few hours.

In the ranks of the national police, they're speaking in hushed tones about a new invention which will contribute greatly to their work. It's the new *Glass Detective Eye*. This artificial eye can of course only be worn by an officer who is already missing an eye.

It resembles an ordinary glass eye, but the *Glass Detective Eye* is actually a little camera equipped with an ordinary photographic plate. Once loaded, the officer inserts the device in a darkroom. He closes the glass eye, opens the good one, and sets off to find the suspect. He positions himself before the suspect, opens the photographic eye, and closes it after the correct exposure time, then returns to the precinct.

His eye is removed in the same darkroom. The film need only be developed to provide a photograph of the suspect. It's a practical invention. It doesn't draw attention to itself, and it only requires a little getting used to on the officer's part.

XII

FINE ARTS — THEATER — THE PRESS

Tableaux Vivants — Pneumatic Cinema Seats — A New Daily Paper: *The Conscience* — Models at the Place Pigalle — Frame for Cubist Paintings — Society for Cinema on the Metro — A Cubist Scandal — Climbing Plants for Carrying Up Letters — Daltonist Salon — Advertising Horseshoes — Leasing Out of Statues — Cinematographic Summaries — *La Maison du Vase Brisé* — The Frantic School — Hermaphrodites at the Theater — The Musicographical Revolver for Casinos

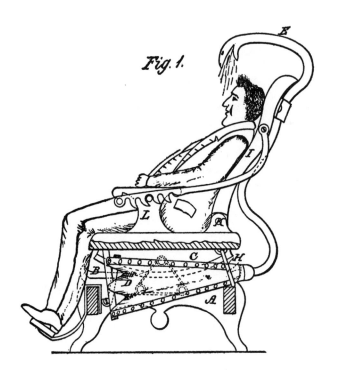

Fig. 1.

The bourgeoisie are too quick to make fun of certain contemporary paintings, without fully understanding the difficulties with which artists are often confronted. Some of them, lacking resources, are forced to rent cut-price apartments on streets where buses rumble by. This causes a slight trembling of the hand visible in their paintings. Others, for lack of capital, must steal canvas from street sweepers and paint with oil leaked from taxis. This imparts a certain crudeness to their works, and at times a displeasing color.

The bourgeoisie are particularly ignorant—this must be said—of the proper way of looking at a modern painting. Thus, laymen laugh stupidly before cubist canvases, simply because they've committed the unpardonable error of hanging them on the wall to display them, as one did with canvases in the olden days. Cubism, at heart, is nothing but the application of cinematography to painting. Thus, the canvas *must be in motion* if the fragmented gestures are to recompose themselves. One of our best-known art lovers understood the problem, and his splendid gallery of *Rotating Paintings* is now one of the wonders of Paris. This gallery is full of *Swivellustrations* that turn on a pivot like the old Kinetoscopes. Along the walls, one sees nymphs bathing, climbing out of the water, entering the baths again; dogs sit up and beg; horses run indefinitely around a racetrack. In a few years, we'll be done with the *tableaux morts* that we currently hang in our salons. People will only want *tableaux vivants* worthy of the name, connected to the electric supply. This is a true revolution in painting. Our art lovers would do well to pay attention.

Until today, cinema managers have complained of the difficulty they have emptying the theater after each showing.

The new *Pneumatic Seats*, made entirely of rubber, put an elegant end to this difficulty.

After each showing, a valve is opened, and the seats deflate. The spectators leave of their own accord, and the seats must merely be reinflated to prepare the theater for the next showing.

Our great daily papers had better look sharp. The founding of a new newspaper has been announced in Paris: *The Conscience* will be perfectly adapted to the needs of modern life, aimed at replacing all existing papers.

The Conscience will be printed on a thin little elastic sheet of white rubber. The printing will be microscopic, allowing the most compact of formats. Thus, *The Conscience* can be easily stuffed into a coat pocket without the wearer worrying about stretching out the garment. This practical quality will be particularly appreciated by the fashion-forward.

Being printed on rubber, one can read *The Conscience* while carrying out one's morning toilet or even taking a bath. This second quality will be extremely appreciated in an era when hygiene makes significant progress each day.

But, you protest, won't these microscopic letters be difficult to read, particularly for those with poor vision? In this you are mistaken! Since the pages are made of elastic rubber, one need simply pull on them to produce letters in the exact size desired. People with good vision need only pull a little on the paper, while those with poor vision can extend it considerably to obtain enormous script. No more reading glasses, no more magnifying glasses for the morning paper! Elderly people will be delighted by *The Conscience*.

In addition, in an age when sports are very popular, this reading exercise will have highly beneficial consequences. The effort exerted by the arms to distend the paper will be an excellent replacement for the *exercise machines* currently being sold. While we're on the subject, we'd like to mention that the *Supplement for Athletes*, printed on extra strong rubber, will be made available to the public. The athlete of course wants to finish their reading by leafing vigorously through the pages with all their strength, completing their training without boredom.

But that's not all: the ink used for *The Conscience* will be made of mustard seed powder, and once it has been read, the paper will make an excellent poultice. Placed on the chest, it will protect against colds and bronchitis. After being used, this poultice can be turned into *excellent fly paper*. One need only place it in a room, and few hours later, you will be rid of these dangerous little beasts.

Is that all? Not yet. The business responsible for *The Conscience* will buy back this fly paper at the sale price, concocting excellent plum puddings with this quarry, to be given to subscribers as a bonus gift.

It's the latest thing in modern journalism, and we're told that the elastic *Conscience* has even more surprises in store for you!

The role of the popular press is truly an admirable one today.

It's astonishing to see how the Place Pigalle has been transformed into a veritable *cour des Miracles*.[24] At the same spot where artists' models once gathered to wait for the painters who would hire them, today one encounters the injured and maimed: the blind, the armless, the legless, unfortunate workers who lost half their face in a machine accident or broke their spine in a belt drive. A quick investigation allowed us to confirm that this was still the model market taking place around the fountain at the Place Pigalle. It's just that painting has evolved in recent years, and new schools have taken precedence; the cubists and futurists are the order of the day. As is clear, they no longer know what to do with the figure of the Holy Father or the Madonna presented to us by the Italian classics. They lacked models appropriate to their genre of painting, and so the character of the model market has transformed radically.

It's a curious sign of the times.

A Rive Gauche picture framer is about to make a fortune with the *New Frame for Cubist Paintings*. Of course, this frame features six completely gilded sides. The work of art is contained within. This method of framing cubist paintings makes them particularly attractive.

The recently founded *Society for Cinema on the Metro* is a matter of publicity, and I would refuse to talk about it in this volume entirely dedicated to pure science, were it not for the fact that this industrial matter is connected to a technical innovation of the most enticing variety.

We've learned that *The Society for Cinema on the Metro* has acquired the legal right to lease the walls of the tunnels between each station. Small glowing images from cinematographic films will be enlarged considerably on these walls, and each glowing image will be separated from its neighbor by a thin black partition. When a subway train speeds between two stations, the travelers can observe the cinematographic scenes in astonished admiration as they play out along the walls of the Metro. Of course—alas!—these scenes will be used to promote some product or other, demonstrating the positive results of using a remedy or lotion. We won't say any more about this commercial side of the matter, but we will point out that this felicitous application of the old Kinetoscopes will bring joy to melancholy Metro travelers.

There's a great scandal brewing among painters, collectors, and art dealers. It seems that certain recently sold cubist and futurist canvasses were simply enlargements of photographs taken with a microscope of a drop of water from the Seine. These colorized enlargements were sold to the public under various titles: *Portrait of Mme X. . .* or *General Y. . .*

It's a known fact that in certain provincial villages far from our feverish Parisian life *climbing plants are used to deliver letters.* When the postman comes by, he attaches the mail to a wisteria, ivy, or Virginia creeper, and sometime later, the letter is hand-delivered to the second floor. It's an astonishing custom for Parisians, but it seems perfectly natural to some country people.

This charming habit will soon be introduced to Paris, where it will beautify the windows of our starry-eyed seamstresses. Climbing plants will carry young girls love letters from their beaus, and its adherents will insist on never receiving mail by another channel. This will also give everyone time to reflect; only the most serious romantic interests will survive this test. The organizers of this matter have thought of everything. Of course, a letter sent in this way will take more time to land in the hands of the young girl living on the seventh floor than a woman who already has a mezzanine apartment.

There will also be pigeons in the gutter eager to snatch up a letter before it arrives at its destination. This practice may seem a bit outdated to skeptical people, a bit "1830." But let us admit that it will bring charm to the frantic life in our big cities.

Life today has become very difficult for painters. Each day they are forced to become more specialized to earn a living. In this vein, the *New Daltonist Salon* will open soon, exhibiting only paintings without red or green, in order to attract amateurs suffering from color blindness.

In addition, works that don't sell at this salon will still be good for the autumn salon, where they will be exhibited under a different guise.

Certain big advertising firms have gotten the idea to write on the asphalt of the street during dry weather, using horses equipped with rubber shoes. But the procedure didn't work because the ink couldn't be easily reapplied to these wet stamps. They solved the problem by seeking vicious horses with the bad habit of constantly kicking. Behind the *Kicking Horse* but in front of the coachman, the usual mud guard will be replaced by a damp ink pad that will refresh the rubber stamps each time the horse kicks. The advertisements will then be printed on the ground a great number of times. One must merely stop the kicking horse, yoked to its carriage, in the middle of a very busy square, and then agitate the animal by pulling back its reins.

Faced with the ever-increasing number of statues erected in Paris, the Municipal Council has decided to erect statues wearing frock coats, seated on a horse or in a chair, with removable heads and inscriptions.

Following the tastes of the day, the hero will be switched out, with each monument granted a ten-year permit. Needless to say, supporters need only pay for the new head and rent for the location of the body.

To satisfy the taste of modern spectators, many of the big popular theaters have hit upon a very practical idea. From now on, the curtain will be replaced with a screen on which a summary of the preceding act will be projected during each intermission. Thus, one can arrive late at the theater without inconvenience. For those spectators from the outlying districts who will need to leave early, there's also the possibility of projecting a summary of the conclusion on the same screen.

Thus transformed, the theater would have no reason to envy the cinema.

For New Year's, the *Maison du Vase Brisé* has requested that we remind its numerous clientele that it has just renewed its important agreements with the big French and Italian manufacturers of porcelain and crystal.[25]

For just a few pennies, the *Maison du Vase Brisé* can always deliver splendid gifts whose value sometimes exceeds several thousand francs.

The *Maison du Vase Brisé* purchases accidentally broken art objects from the grand manufacturers; it adroitly boxes up the pieces and sends them to the address of the person to whom one would like to give a gift.

Its special deliverymen, admirably trained, act as though they are extremely drunk, and no one is surprised when they open the box only to find the priceless art object has broken into a thousand pieces. Thus, for a very modest sum, one can seem to have sent an expensive item, and everyone is satisfied.

The *Maison du Vase Brisé* has also requested that we discreetly remind its clientele not to fear the irritating errors that occurred last year: the fragments of certain objects were wrapped too carefully, with each one in a separate piece of paper. It was a warehouse error which certainly won't be repeated this year.

The *Frantic School* will be the great success of the exposition of the Society of Independent Artists this year, with many noteworthy entries.

Frantic painters refuse to hang their canvasses on walls, therefore rendering them immobile. Frantic canvasses will be displayed on the backs of special porters, selected from notorious alcoholics or sufferers of Saint Vitus Dance.

The Frantic School claims to adhere to the Bergsonian theories that are so fashionable right now. It doesn't consider painting to be a static state, and the motionless stammerings of cubism only make it sneer.

Frantic painters depend on the porter's constant motion to mix the lines and colors, producing the desired effect, a little like a cinematograph. It's among the most interesting of experiments, one which perfectly characterizes our modern painting and philosophy, but which above all complicates the task of the collector.

Fortunately, the matter is no problem at all. We've just learned that the great collectors of modern painting have had the excellent idea to rent apartments on streets where certain buses pass by each day. The paintings on the walls in these new galleries will be constantly in motion, responding to the Bergsonian desires expressed by the new *Frantic School*.

It's certainly added value that the owners of the buildings didn't take into consideration.

Rumors have been confirmed that the Comédie-Française will present several new pieces featuring a curious character who has been far too neglected in the theater up to now. I'm talking about the *hermaphrodite.* When only men and women were used, dramatic situations were always the same. The hermaphrodite can change their sex according to the act, and the new pieces will present an infinite variety of situations, with a truly impressive surprise factor.

There's a new trend making waves at the moment, and which certain snobs would like to introduce here for the summer season. It consists in firing a revolver a few times into the partition which stands before the orchestra conductor in seaside casinos and elegant cafes. The adept conductor must play (or rather have played) the unexpected note thus implanted in his music as the hole left by the revolver bullet. When the note is played to their satisfaction, the spectators' enthusiasm knows no bounds, and the conductor immediately receives a significant reward.

This behavior may be highly amusing in America, but please allow us to say that it's out of place in a civilized nation.

XIII

ANTHROPOLOGY — ETHNOGRAPHY —

THE OCCULT — TRAVEL

The Soldier of Marathon — The Benedisiphon — The Human Butcher — Illuminated Wallace Fountains — Sheet-Metal Lamp Glass — Useful Statues — Rotating Slabs for Prussians — Colorized Phantoms — Our Forerunner the Crab — The Materialization of Beef Steaks

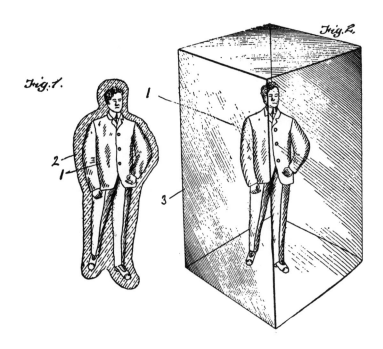

Fig. 1.

Fig. 2.

Did you know that the famous soldier of Marathon was lame? An expert report presented to the Academy of Humanities has informed us about the matter.

It seems that lame people actually run faster than others because their shorter leg causes them to fall rapidly forward. Only a lame person could have accomplished this endeavor. This scientific observation is worthy of note. While we're on the subject, we deny the legend that the soldier of Marathon was the first Greek deserter.

The *Benedisiphon* is a luxury item that with time will replace the old holy water sprinkler in our great Parisian churches. Its exterior form resembles that sacred instrument precisely. A press button allows the sophisticated public to use the device like a siphon, with the same precision and the same control. As we can see, the church is modernizing.

Many people have sent urgent requests asking me to explain the *New Human Butcher* that just opened on a large boulevard. Within the red gates of this fantastic butcher's shop, dismayed pedestrians can observe the fragments of human bodies suspended on hooks: arms, legs, heads lined up on marble slabs.

Let us reassure our readers. These human remains are made of wax, and it is merely an American publicity stunt, and a bold one at that, which is sure to cause a stir. In a few days, posters will advise the public that "not buying Globales Depurative Capsules is like giving your body to the butcher," and the crowd will have gotten itself worked up over nothing.

Beginning next month in Paris we'll see the new *Illuminated Wallace Fountains*. A great American philanthropist, president of many societies combating alcoholism, has given the city of Paris the necessary sums to transform all the old fountains from the good Mr. Wallace.[26] A red electric projection will color the jet of water from the Wallace fountains at night, recalling the most seductive shades of a well-aged burgundy wine. Drunkards attracted by this spectacle will abandon the cabaret and rush to the Wallace fountains, to their great benefit. Given their complete inebriation, it's hoped that they won't notice the substitution and will take a water cure more to their liking than those in our health resorts.

An explorer has told us of the *Sheet Metal Lamp Glass* used in bars in America. The sheet metal is used, not as one might think, as an act of economy replacing fragile glass that doesn't withstand brawls, but because the sheet metal produces total darkness which prevents the fighters from attacking each other. On calmer days, the ordinary sheet metal can be replaced with white silver-lined metal for illumination.

The statues of various philanthropists that adorn our public squares will soon be modified in an ingenious way. Hinges will be added to their frock coats, forming the doors of cabinets where street laborers can easily store their brooms. Sand, poured into their legs, can be collected for use in traffic through the opened soles of their shoes. The statues will finally be good for something.

In the little Prussian villages, everyone is talking about the new rotating slabs that the municipalities have started to place at each end of the road. Thus, on Sundays the bourgeois families will be freed from the uncertainty and effort of having to change direction. Once they arrive at the end of the sidewalk, they stand on the rotating slab, which is activated by a simple spring. Then they can take up their walk in the opposite direction, without disrupting the absolute linearity of their stroll.

✿

In certain circles there's a lot of talk about dyeing phantoms using aniline vapors. Colorized phantoms have already been used with success as stage decorations in some Parisian theaters. They could also be used to fill the Chamber of Deputies in the morning.[27] It's a very curious scientific discovery whose applications could be numerous. Starting now, the railway companies have instructed their employees that voyagers wishing to be seated alone may not fill their compartments with colorized phantoms.

Science is full of disconcerting surprises. Who would have thought even just a few years ago that phantoms would be put to daily use, that they would be domesticated.

Each day naturalists reveal to us anew how humanity, despite its pretensions, hasn't really invented much; animals, even the most inferior kinds, are often far ahead of us, and they know from instinct what people discover only after extensive inquiry.

We've all noticed how hackney coachmen warm themselves on their bench in winter by hitting their biceps in cadence with the palms of their hands. And would you believe it, crabs have done the same thing since the dawn of time; a report given to the Academy of Science presented the evidence.

A naturalist on an early holiday observed the phenomenon on a Norman beach. When it got cold and the crabs on the sand were exposed to a frosty wind, they crossed their claws in front of them and tapped their arms just like our brave hackney coachmen.

Yet another civilized gesture that doesn't belong to us at all.

Until now, our most reputable mediums have only been able to accomplish materializations of bouquets, flowers, heads of the deceased, or little wisps unsuitable for any use.

Thanks to recent accomplishments on the part of a large charitable society, several mediums, given appropriate preparation, were able to materialize pasta, beef steaks, and chickens. These products of spiritualism were distributed to needy families in the poorer quarters.

That's a practical application of spiritualism, which will convince skeptics more rapidly than long arguments. At the same time, the gesture has an elegance that all philanthropists will appreciate.

XIV

PURE AND APPLIED SCIENCE

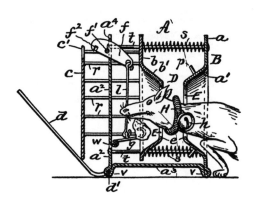

Whatever poets might have said about the moon, we must admit that until now this nocturnal body has remained absolutely useless, and that its uselessness has grown to be a scandal in the mechanized, utilitarian world in which we live.

We hope that this ridiculous poetic anomaly will be put to an end thanks to the prodigious efforts of a film production company that is currently considering a truly colossal project that will benefit a large English watchmaking firm.

Using a light source of previously unknown intensity, the production company will cinematographically project the image of a clock onto the lunar dial, so that terrestrials can see the time all through the night. Of course, the movement of the device will be such that the projection follows the course of the moon. Greenwich time will be displayed.

We hardly need enumerate the enormous benefits that such a nocturnal clock would bring to thousands of people. We only regret that the firm that created this astounding projection saw fit to inscribe its name in the middle of the dial. It's simply a necessity of modern advertising we're forced to accept. And when you think of the grandiose results of such an enterprise, it's easy to put it out of your mind.

The *Travel Alarm-Clock Chronopulse* will be highly appreciated by all explorers who spend many long months far from clocks, as well as those unfortunate people who cannot purchase an ordinary watch.

The extremely affordable *Chronopulse* is placed on the wrist, similar to a sports watch with a leather strap. It is activated by the beating of the pulse, which powers an escapement just like in a typical watch.

Without a complicated mechanism or a spring prone to breakage, the watch runs as long as its wearer lives. Though it may be a bit macabre, it also will exactly indicate the wearer's time of death. The *Chronopulse* can also function as an alarm clock, always useful for business travelers.

A large pencil factory has begun specially training several thousand of those intelligent insects known as *woodworms*, which chew holes in wood and have found themselves without employment since antique furniture sellers replaced their services with the faster method of firing buckshot at heirlooms. As you may have guessed, the worms are used by pencil makers to drill a hole through the wood precisely where the lead will be placed. They care for the worms and choose those which are of the exact caliber of the lead to be inserted.

The interesting thing about this little invention is how easy it is to make the worms bore through the wood in a perfectly straight line. One must simply stuff the worm into the end of the pencil with great force. Since the wood is of superior quality, its density is very consistent and the worm isn't tempted to tunnel to the left or right, because no easier route is to be found there. Quite to the contrary; turning would represent more work for it, so the worm continues straight on, never deviating from its route. This procedure is of a childlike simplicity, as you can see, but it still had to be discovered.

The manufacturer has just been granted a twenty-year patent on this idea, and they've capped it off with yet another discovery. Not only does the worm bore through the wood, but a piece of lead is attached to its tail with a thread, so that when its work is done, the lead has already been inserted in the pencil. One must merely snip its little thread and the worm is ready to work again.

Unfortunately, we must note that the Society for the Protection of Animals has once again gotten involved in these matters. Through an intermediary at the police precinct, it made it known to the involved parties that this treatment seemed barbaric and urged them to use little harnesses for pulling the lead. It also demanded goggles for the worms so that they wouldn't be blinded by wood splinters. Isn't that pushing their love of animals a bit far?

For all sportsmen, we'd like to highlight the *Cigar Umbrella*, a little wonder of smithery and mechanics.

This little umbrella, which is very light and of minuscule dimensions, is held on the cigar with a ring. Its base is equipped with a little jack situated on a piece of expandable metal on castors, which allow the ring to be progressively drawn back.

When the lit end of the cigar draws near, the metal expands, the umbrella draws back, and the metal contracts, ready to expand once again.

The entire ensemble is extremely lightweight and won't disturb one's afternoon stroll. The cigar burns down to its end without being put out by the rain.

The *Anti-Vermin Reverberation Apparatus* is a new trap for flies and mosquitoes based on a highly scientific concept. Its practical utility is particularly praiseworthy. It consists of a noise-emitting device which releases vibrations that *conflict* with those generated by the wings of flies. The fly, *thrown off its stride* as one says of bicycle racers, falls to the ground, dragging itself along pitifully, and the heel of a shoe does the rest.

The *Anti-Vermin Reverberation Apparatus* can also be used conveniently at any time as an instrument in the orchestration of a piece of modern music, or as a car horn. It thus unites work with pleasure.

If we are to believe a recent report made at the Academy of Science, *Black Light* has been definitively discovered. It's easy to foresee the extraordinary consequences that projections of *Black Light* could have; in war for example, to conceal entire regiments. Unfortunately, real *Black Light* has one grave fault: by altering light waves, they are transformed into sound waves, and it seems that *Black Light* makes a terrible racket. Let's hope that new advances will soon eliminate this practical inconvenience.

Photographers are in a state of commotion. No more time-consuming and costly retouching, no more precise and unflattering portraits that discourage clientele. By means of little projectors which cast variously colored rays onto this or that part of the face, the client's face will be *retouched* in advance, while they are posing. It's a little like in a certain Montmartre cabaret where a serene face is transformed into a skull. Except in the photographer's studio, just the opposite occurs. With a bit of dexterity, even the ugliest people are transformed: a nose straightened, eyes enlarged, mouth shaped. These photographs, which are *based on nature*, don't require any retouching, and the enthusiasm of the clientele will be its own reward.

Our snobs are overjoyed. An international conference has just been convened to standardize the direction of screw threads on monocles. Until now, English monocles screwed in to the left and French monocles to the right, causing great headaches for suppliers. The counterclockwise English variant will probably be adopted for all nations. Ultimately, this will please the fashionable among us and won't harm anyone.

In the twentieth century, no one would recommend that bookkeepers write the number twelve in the following fashion: IIIIIIIIIIII. That's an approach we abandoned back in the stone age.

The eye immediately grasps the number twelve when written "12"; and yet the same doesn't go for the ear. It's much weaker than those of animals, and on public clocks, it can only recognize the hour by means of separate tones: *ding, ding, ding, ding, ding, ding, ding, ding, ding, ding, ding, ding*—to spell it out—when one just wants to express a simple idea: *noon* or *midnight*!

This unspeakable vestige of barbarism has justifiably upset a young Scotch music lover, who has proposed that we replace this old iteration of the hours, which is necessarily repetitive, by playing one note of the scale from high to low each hour from morning to night: *do, ti, la, sol, fa, me, re, do, ti, la, sol, fa* . . .

According to this system, noon would be *fa*, and midnight would be expressed by the same note played twice in a lower tone: *fa fa*. It would be very easy for the ear to recognize the notes, which would get lower and lower as the day went on, and which would rise sharply in pitch, clear and high, beginning at one in the morning. No doubt this system will soon be adopted for all public clocks. It would also nicely complement the musical education given to young French people.

Our jewelers are delighted. They've just invented a new double ring for rolling marbles, with one ring worn on each thumb. If well fitted, this new device allows the wearer to twiddle their thumbs for hours on end without the least fatigue or danger of overheating. We are convinced that this new fashion will be welcomed by out-of-work retirees.

The *New Pocket Ruler Measuring Only One Inch* is a lovely little invention, simple yet clever. To use it, just place it over the object in question twelve times to obtain the length in feet. This portable ruler will be appreciated by architects, masons, and painters who until now were obligated to carry ungainly rulers around with them.

The new *Writing Gloves* made of rubber are revolutionizing the world of typing. These molded rubber gloves have the letters of the alphabet, the numbers, and the punctuation marks in relief on the tip of each finger. Don this pair of gloves and you can immediately write without having to use a cumbersome typewriter. The most commonly used letters are at the very tips of the fingers, with the others arranged below them; the least commonly used characters are placed above the nail and are printed with a bent finger. Ink is supplied by a stamp pad at the palm of the glove. Simply make a fist after typing each line to ink up all the characters. Only the exclamation point is located on the side of the hand. It is printed by striking the paper with a closed fist. This new system demands great precision for the characters to be printed neatly in place. But this precision can be achieved in a few weeks of practice, and from that point on, the user has the valuable advantage of this new procedure, which allows them to type while traveling with just a pair of gloves tucked handily into their pocket.

For wet weather, the new *Rotating Illuminated Umbrella* is on sale everywhere. This umbrella very much resembles ordinary umbrellas, with the difference that its frame is mounted on bearings and can turn freely, powering a tiny generator that feeds a little electric lamp in the handle. At night, during storms, or in high winds, the umbrella rotates, generating the energy for lamplight. It's an invention that will be well received, especially in the countryside.

We knew that the railway companies' recent reform of the hour indicated on their schedules wouldn't be the last we heard of such improvements. Noting the hours from zero to twenty-four still calls for recourse to supplementary numbers for the minutes, and completely neglects the seconds. One must admit that this system is extremely outdated and unscientific. Beginning 1 September, the railway signs won't mention the *hour* of the given day, but simply the exact *second*, the sidereal day being composed, as we know, of 86,400 seconds. With the old system, one said for example: "Take the 8:47 train, which will let you off at Saint-Mihil at 9:22." Today we say: "Take the 20:47 train, which will let you off at Saint-Mihil at 21:22." Tomorrow things will be much simpler. We'll just say: "Take the 74,820 train, which will let you off at Saint-Mihil at 76,920." A single number will suffice to indicate the exact second of the day. We'll no longer say: "What's the hour?" but rather, "What's the second?" It's a reform that truly suits our era of exactitude and precision.

However, this simplified reform intended for the wider public cannot suffice for our scientists. On this topic, I recently received a very interesting letter from the Bureau des Longitudes dated "Paris, 60,308,722,800 *seconds*."[28] It seems that from now on in the world of science, they intend to note the year, month, day, hour, minute, and second in one single number. Thus, instead of saying "Take the 74,820 train on 15 September, which will let you off at Saint-Mihil at 76,920," we'll soon be saying "Take the 60,325,961,220 train, which will let you off at Saint-Mihil at 60,325,963,320." This new notation, based on *the second of the Christian era*, will bring great precision to our daily lives. It could be used in correspondence or in business. However, we must note that this reform could be applied to railway schedules only on the sole condition that a new schedule be published *each day*, which is no small task. There is also a new notation, but only for specialists, still based on the Christian era *but in fifths of a second*, for the timing of important sporting events. It's another simplification brought about through scientific reforms.

The Italians have just announced a lovely little invention: the *Tip Guard for Mosquitoes*. This tip guard is constructed from those little glass beads found in shops, whose central hole is stuffed with a simple mixture of pitch and ground beef. Simply scatter the little beads, thus equipped, on the furniture in a room. A mosquito lands on a bead, sinks its stinger into the beef, and the stinger remains stuck in the pitch. Thus, the mosquito is equipped with a tip guard, rendering it inoffensive. It can fly about as it likes, and nothing is prettier than the sun reflecting off thousands of mosquitoes adorned with multicolored beads.

There's a lot of talk in the world of engineering about the *New Barometric Funicular* they're building between Lake Geneva and the Rochers de Naye. This new mountain railway is genial. Constructed like other funiculars, it has room for two cars, one climbing and one descending, connected by a cable that wraps around a drum at the summit. It will also include a little wooden ladder parallel to the tracks and running from the lake to the peak.

When the weather is nice countless barometrically sensitive frogs that normally stay around the lake will cling to the rungs of the ladder. Once they arrive at the summit, these frogs will be placed in the descending car under the careful direction of an employee. They will then form the necessary counterweight to lift the rising car. What's more, the frogs are merely an extra push since the weight of the descending passengers must ultimately equal that of those ascending.

It's a very pleasing way to put the frogs' special instincts to work, which drive them to climb ladders when the weather is nice. Since the funicular is only intended for tourists, it doesn't matter if it stops running in bad weather, on those days when the frogs refuse to render their services.

All anyone is talking about in the world of industry this year is the new gas that's to compete with lean gas in powering small domestic motors. It's the new *Wretched Gas*, obtained from the waste products of residual alcohol, whose cost to the consumer is truly minimal. It's said that wretched gas will be within everyone's means, even the most modest, and that ragpickers can use it to power their little carts. It will also be used for all domestic purposes, as well as in the poorhouses. We'll wait before making up our minds on the matter.

GASTON DE PAWLOWSKI

✿

A more elegant subject, better suited to charm tender souls, is a lovely little invention by a gentlewoman whose name we won't mention in order to preserve her modesty, and which will be used in all local schools next academic year. It's the little lead *Toast Balancer*, which one sticks into the bread on the side opposite the one being buttered or, depending on the circumstances, covered in jam.

Until now, when the toast fell to the floor, as is customary, the weight of the condiments always made it fall butter-side-down in the dust. That has disastrous consequences for young children's stomachs, who immediately devour all that microbe-infested dirt and dust. The *Toast Balancer* has eliminated this danger; the lead weight always pulls the correct side of the toast downward and our children's health is safeguarded along with their jam.

XV

MORES AND CUSTOMS —

PRIVATE LIFE — FOLKLORE

The Misunderstood Lesson — Poultice Handkerchiefs — The Sunday Hatchet — Drop-Cover Pajamas — Camel Stools — Bell Barometer for Drunkards — Device for Drying Tears — The Boomerang Gift — Gifts for Children — Communications Alarm — Trapdoor Chair — Crab Nutcracker — The Smiler

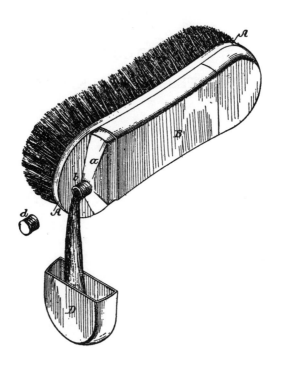

Do-gooder newspapers have gotten hold of a terrible incident that recently ravaged an entire small suburban town. Students sitting calmly on the railing of a bridge failed to help a wretch disappearing into the waters of the river, and instead mocked him together, sticking out their tongues in cadence, without even thinking to notify the local waterway company.

This incident more than sufficed to recriminate the state school system and the education that it provides. Upon further inquiry, it was just a regrettable and embarrassing error. During a lesson, the schoolmaster explained to the children that to bring a drowned person back to life, one must move the tongue rhythmically, but the children misunderstood whose tongue the schoolmaster was referring to and these poor little ones did everything in their power to save the drowning man by sticking out their tongues.

A large burial firm (embalming, inquiries into wills on behalf of families, exhumations, funeral meals, etc.) informed us that from now on, it will make special *Poultice Handkerchiefs* available to its clientele. Discreetly coated with mustard powder, these kerchiefs will allow the heirs to cry copiously during the ceremony without having to try.

This could prove useful when one party wants to contest the will, and we are convinced that these new handkerchiefs will be warmly welcomed by all those concerned for their dignity.

Among all the new fashions, we must take note of a practical little hatchet, which busy bachelors can wear on their belts on Sundays. As you may have guessed, this hatchet is used to hack a path through the families that hold hands and completely block our grand avenues. It may seem a bit extreme, but if we're honest, it's the only way if you have an urgent errand to run.

Among the innovations in high society this year, the new *Drop-Cover Pajamas for Morning Meetings* have an elegant character. These pajamas in waxed cotton are like the covers thrown over golden chandeliers in the countryside, and they completely cover the face and body of the wearer. They allow for morning meetings with favor-seekers and nuisances free of fatigue, and the host can sleep if need be while the guest talks, all without the latter noticing. What's more, this little number indicates clearly that this should not be an extended visit. It's a discreet hint; it is to the soul what normal drop covers are to furniture.

Recently we've all seen those camel stools they've been using in the bigger bars. The new *Articulated Camel Stool* kneels when you want to climb up on it, and to get it to rise again, one need only give it a few kicks in the hooves. This innovation will soon also be applied to automobiles and luxury trains, which will be equipped with articulated iron cable wheels. Thus, we'll have *camel cars* and *camel trains* that kneel to allow travelers to mount them and then get back up.

Will improvements to our comfort ever cease?

For fashionable night owls who return home in a state of intoxication, we recommend the new *Precision Chronometer-Barometer*. This barometer arrives perfectly calibrated. It rings a bell when the night owl has arrived at the floor of their residence in the dark. The precision barometer indicates the altitude, activating the bell, alerting those in the apartment that the night owl needs help if they have fallen against the door.

The new *Device for Drying Tears* consists of an adorable little pocket kit that includes a little stuffed monkey mounted on a pince-nez, along with a pocket mirror. A quick look in the mirror will be all it takes to stop crying, considering how ridiculous the little monkey looks perched on the bridge of one's nose. It's the best that science has to offer in these matters.

What anguish and uncertainty awaits us in the final days of the year when we must buy a thousand little useless, charming trinkets to delight our friends for the holidays. Often one even gives in to despair and offers a friend a gift which one has just received from another friend. The *Boomerang* is a new little gift specially invented for this purpose, and which can circulate from hand to hand, as the name indicates, returning to its originator without causing chagrin, all while pleasing everybody. This gift is special in that it can be given on a thousand different occasions, being reused indefinitely. In short, it is a *Cigar-Case Brooch* made of amber that can be embellished with diamonds.

It's constructed in such a way that it can be given as a pencil sharpener, an umbrella case, a telephone chart folder, a penholder, a little diorama, an ear swab, or a dog whistle. Between the 8th and 10th of January, when it arrives with its final beneficiary, it can be used as an irrigation cannula. As you can see, it's a gift anyone would be eager to receive. It simplifies the search and eliminates hesitation at a time of year when it's particularly difficult to come up with ideas.

This year they've finally decided to sell *real toys* that will delight the children who receive them and not just the adults who buy them. In this spirit, the new *Tilting Soup Bowls* are on sale everywhere. The slightest nudge is enough to send them plummeting to the floor if they are full. There are also *Perforated Cups*, which allow wine to pool on the tablecloth, as well as *Nasal Dilators* which bear some resemblance to glove openers. In addition, there is the *Salon Shooter*, a crossbow that launches flaming pegs at the shutters, where they stick by means of a spike. The *Little Lead Winter Sports Figurines* will also be appreciated. They can be stuck by means of little cleat onto the bald heads of paralyzed grandfathers. Delightful mountain climbing scenes can be composed in this way, depicting the ascent of a glacier.

These modern toys will delight our little angels, especially the new *Nasal Finger Made of Molded Blotting Paper with Optional Celluloid Nails for Nail Biters*. This new toy is clean and discreet. It is sold in a box of twelve and will be particularly appreciated by parents who worry about their children's health. The children, for their part, will be delighted by this new invention because the Nasal Finger is constructed in such a fashion that it allows the nostrils to be dilated to twice their normal size.

We would also like to mention the new *Sitting-Room Stream with Sterilized Mud, Enriched with Calcium Phosphate*. This new little brook for the sitting room is entirely constructed of carefully welded zinc. It is waterproof and won't stain the carpet. It's an endless source of entertainment for young children when bad weather keeps them inside.

Also to be noted is the *Pipe-Piercing Augur Game* for the bathtub with eggs to be placed on the jet of water for target practice; the *Headquarters Wire-Cutter Game* with everything required for sabotage, including two telegraph posts and replacement wires all carefully packaged in a box; and the *Nautical Catastrophe Model Railroad Set* with corpses to be discovered, all in good taste and sure to delight the little devils of today.

At a time when the spirit of the family is weakening with each passing day, we're pleased to announce *The New Sabotage Kit for Invalid Grandparents*, also known as the *Amateur Detective Kit* with funnel for pouring water down someone's collar, pepper for their eyes, rope restraints, and handcuffs. What could be more praiseworthy than to tighten the familial ties that bind grandparents and the grandchildren they adore?

Most Parisians who want to wake up early are in the habit of sending themselves an urgent telegram in the evening via pneumatic tube, which is abruptly announced to them in the wee hours of the morning by a little telegraph girl. Obviously, there are simpler ways. If you have a telephone, you can have one of your employees wake you up with a phone call from the office. At least that saves the telegraph girl a useless disruption. Unfortunately, until now, this morning alarm system was not allowed by the government. Beginning next February, by means of a special tax limited to twenty cents, all telephone owners can be awoken by an office employee, by sending a special unstamped postcard to the State Undersecretary of Communications, who will confirm it within a fortnight. It's an excellent innovation, which does service to the quality of our bureaucracy.

We've received several notices about a new and very practical invention: the *Revolver-Style Trapdoor Chair* for university presidents distributing prizes or other academic honors. This rocking chair has two sides. When the spectators' attention is on the laureate, the chair rocks, and a dummy dressed in the same robe, cap, and honorific garb as the president takes his place while the real president disappears through a trapdoor and can proceed to the refreshments table while the ceremony continues. It's very practical, very simple, and it safeguards all appearances.

Housewives are thrilled. In Paris they're selling a fashionable new nutcracking crab whose careful training will earn it a place on every elegant table. Nothing is more amusing than to see the crab obligingly crack the nuts and almonds handed to it after dinner. The crab goes about its work with all the more enthusiasm because it knows that dessert poses no immediate threat to it, and that the guests aren't salivating over its unhappy demise. It's an innocent pleasure that will cheer up long, official dinner parties this winter.

Now here is a sad invention that we believe could find great success in our contemporary society. *The Smiler* is particularly recommended for industrialists and businessmen who struggle to meet the needs of a beloved luxury-minded woman, despite their dogged work, and who would like to conceal their fatigue and anguish from her.

The Smiler consists of a little variable-tension spring that is inserted in the mouth and held between the cheeks. The wearer can regulate the tension of the smile-force depending on the character of the lady to be pleased. With a bit of tact, one can quickly ascertain the degree of smile that suffices to resolutely welcome the announcement of new and excessive expenses, just as one can determine the level of tension that must not be exceeded to avoid a smile described by the lady as *exasperating* or *idiotic*, and which is followed by a nervous breakdown.

The Smiler arrives in a little cardboard box, ready for insertion. It is available in two models: one for faces that are fatigued and emaciated from overwork, and another for bloated faces. It can also be used by anxious financiers who would like to inspire confidence in their clientele.

We would also like to note in passing that it can be removed very easily in the event of a suicide or accident and saved for a successor.

The nickel-plated steel model is perfectly sufficient for every-day use. The thinly gilded model is more stylish and will be all the more tempting to poor people accustomed to luxury.

XVI

MEDICINE — SURGERY

We're pleased to inform our less fortunate readers of the new *Elastic Dentures for Poor Families*.

These dentures, composed of thirty-two artificial teeth, are mounted on false gums made of red rubber. Members of the same family with different-sized mouths can take turns using them. Depending on what the day calls for, visits to be made, activities to be undertaken, the dentures pass from mouth to mouth, stretching to fit each one's needs.

It's very economical, especially since bad teeth tend to run in families.

For those unfortunates who cannot afford to buy *Elastic Dentures for Poor Families*, a *Discount Model for Very Poor Families* can put the dentures within their reach. It only has six teeth, generally sufficient for a limited diet in these expensive days.

We know how uncomfortable the rubbing of their shirt collar is for people afflicted with boils in springtime. A large shirtmaker has just created collar valves, which are sensitive to the pressure of boils, imitating the safety valve of a steam engine, with the difference being that no fuel is required because all the boiling is carried out by the wearer. The client must merely send a pattern indicating exactly where the boils are located. A few days later, they will receive a *Valve Collar* with perforations that relieve pressure on the boils. A dangerous buildup of pressure and frustration is thus avoided, and another modern safety measure has been put in place. *The wearer can let off steam.* It's a small invention that may seem trivial, but it soothes people who are suffering, and an invention is never frivolous if it diminishes, even in some small sense, the sum of human misery.

Employees of the public welfare system have been delighted with the results of a test of the *New Radiator Bed* currently in a trial run at a large Paris hospital. A current of cold air passes through the tubes of a radiator placed under the sheets of the ill. The water temperature rises and can be used to heat other rooms, where sick people with lower temperatures are shivering. I can think of nothing more touching than this democratic procedure, which will warm our cold hospitals a bit.

Under the rather baffling title *Contribution to a Study of a Possible Use of Gastropods for Operating on Appendicitis*, one of our leading surgeons has presented a truly extraordinary discovery to the Academy of Medicine. He has once more shown the degree of perfection our modern surgical art has attained.

We know that since ancient times, slug syrup has been sold by pharmacists to heal sore throats.[29] Recently this age-old process has been perfected by science. It was remarked that slug syrup had nearly no curative properties, and that it was preferable to use *Living Slugs* whose secretions retain all their restorative values.

Thus, scientists had the idea to feed slugs licorice wood for several weeks, and then to make the ill person eat some lettuce. The ill person swallows the slug, which is attracted by the scent of the lettuce and instinctively glides down the throat, depositing soothing licorice syrup on the walls of the pharynx. To expel the slug, simply put a few fresh lettuce leaves in the ill person's mouth, but this is usually unnecessary because the sick person usually feels a childish disgust at the slug, and generally will expel them all on their own.

You'll have to forgive me for going into these medical details. It's necessary to go over them to explain the new invention presented to the Academy of Medicine.

* * *

In the case of appendicitis, and in general when any perforation of the intestine is apparent, it is very difficult to ligature the perforation from the interior because countless precautions are necessary during the operation to prevent infection. If, even provisionally, one could cover the hole in the intestine *from within*, the operation would be much easier. To accomplish this feat, a leading surgeon had the idea to use *an ordinary medical slug*—used only for sore throats until now—modified with strategic feeding.

The *Surgical Slug* is fed nitrocellulose along with ether and alcohol, and it naturally secretes collodion.[30] The slug is chased into the stomach and then into the intestine by following it with various foods that it hates, and it flees as fast as it can to get them behind it.

When it arrives in the intestine, the desperate slug tries to avoid the hated substances by any means possible. At that moment, the surgeon intervenes and opens the abdomen, and a slender ray of light filters into the intestine through the little hole that he wishes to close. The slug immediately dashes toward this tiny hole to escape, and though it can't fit, it secretes all the collodion it contains in its frenzied attempts. In just a few minutes, the perforation in the intestine is completely sealed *from within* and the operation can be completed without the slightest risk. The slug is then evacuated by ordinary means.

It's an inexpensive, infinitely simple procedure that may seem childish to many people, but which could revolutionize operating techniques for appendicitis the world over.

We're pleased to announce the new *Fever Kit* now on sale in all good pharmacies. This kit is available for a very reasonable price and contains little lightweight pieces of scenery painted on silk, representing views of the desert, palms, camels, and occasionally a lion. Simply hang the scenery around the sick person's bed, and they will immediately be transported into the enchanted lands of the Orient. Instead of suffering from a 104-degree fever, the ill person finds it quite natural and ceases to complain.

Instructions found in the kit also indicate what can be given to the sick person for the duration of their fever. A thrifty housewife can feed a feverish person the scraps of old boots, vinegar, or Tripoli powder. It's a true money saver for the otherwise unfortunate housewife. In winter, this little kit will put Egypt within everyone's reach; it transforms the most terrible illnesses into leisure trips.

An orthopedist from Berlin has started a new trend. It seems he managed to graft *Nickel-Plated Chrome Calluses* onto the ball of the foot, rendering it absolutely skidproof. Anyone equipped with these calluses is guaranteed not to fall in the bathtub or slip on a slick board at the pool. This Kraut invention will no doubt find much success among Austrogoth bathers, but we very much doubt that our fashionable people will decide to adopt it.

Purgative Grass is a very modern innovation that has been sold in all the pharmacies for some time now. This grass is cultivated on airfields. Throughout the year, it is sprinkled with castor oil, which seeps from airplane engines. That's where it gets its medicinal properties, it's no pharmaceutical mystery.

From the dawn of civilization, the corns on our feet have been considered a heavy burden weighing down the forward march of humanity. Thanks to the marvels of modern surgery, the corns on our feet can be skillfully cultivated and ingeniously transplanted, making them a true blessing. Some time ago, they began transplanting the roots of the corn into the pockmarks left on certain people's faces by the ravages of smallpox. The tests were a great success, the corns filled the pockmarks entirely. One need only file them from time to time to obtain beautiful, firm, even skin. We can agree it's a true surgical wonder that will make many people happy.

The latest volume of a new medical journal, *European Taurus*, whose charming, mythological title is a topic all its own, has given us interesting details on feeding children and the preservation of milk. The new *Square Milk Bottle* is a highly ingenious little invention designed to prevent milk from ever turning during transport; they can also be loaded more efficiently into the milk car discussed earlier. One can easily imagine that this new square bottle will be adopted by all those parents who worry about their babies' health.

The same journal also noted—and this will be of interest to wet nurses—the new *Rubber Single-Stream Bosom Amalgamator* can be attached to a nurse's chest without difficulty, uniting the two normally distinct sources of milk into a single feeding bottle. Buridan's baby no longer need hesitate between two equally tempting feasts, and the nurse isn't perpetually imbalanced by the withdrawals made, either on the right or on the left. What's more, it seems that this lack of balance is responsible for the sudden shifts in mood so common in nurses. Parents who have had to suffer these sudden caprices will welcome this invention with pleasure.

For some time now, American dentists have been removing bad teeth using little cartridges of dynamite. Several people have asked us if these explosions don't represent a danger. We're happy to reassure them without hesitation. The explosion of the dynamite is absolutely harmless, on the condition that one isn't in the vicinity at the moment of detonation.

Much progress has been made since the primitive traps for tape-worms patented in 1854. Need we remind you of the creation of the great *Metrotaenia Company* of Liverpool at that time,[31] which captured two thousand tapeworms annually in little round bottles in which they wound themselves automatically around a central spring, unwittingly marking themselves with a line every centimeter by means of an ingenious mechanism designed for this purpose. Thus rolled and metered, the worm is sold as a tape measure for dressmakers. It's nearly indestructible.

The powerful English company's firm monopoly on tapeworms causes terrible difficulties for pharmacists looking to acquire one to decorate their shop. For pharmacists who absolutely must have a tapeworm in a jar to brighten up their front window or hearth, might we suggest that they consider an ordinary, well-worn dressmaker's tape measure with the centimeter marks scrubbed off. Many pharmacists have taken this measure and are completely satisfied. The illusion is perfect.

Among the numerous ancient ideas put forth again by the Committee for Hygiene tasked with combating epidemics, we must first and foremost cite the rat trap called the *Marble Autoverminator*. All the great epidemics are transmitted by rats, so it's valuable to know how to get rid of these dangerous animals quickly and in a practical manner.

The *Marble Autoverminator*, sometimes called *Concussive Rodenticide* in the manuals, simply consists of a pretty, white marble tablet, with or without funerary inscription, which one places flat on the ground. Lay a little bit of lard in the middle of this tablet, dusted with some snuff. The rat is sure to rush to the bait as soon as it sees it. Inevitably, it will sniff up a bit of snuff and be seized by the urgent need to sneeze. With a single sudden blow, it smashes its skull into the marble tablet. What's more, this device is approved by the Society for the Protection of Animals because the rat dies accidentally and is not crushed by a mechanism.

People all over have been asking me for information about the new *Self-Soap* that's causing a big commotion in England. Let's not overstate the matter: our French laboratories of experimental physiology became familiar with the phenomenon several months ago. It's simply the *New Method of Saponification for Adipose Persons*, which will astound people everywhere and delight the overweight.

Expertly portioned subcutaneous injections of soda, potassium, and other substances—all rendered harmless to the patient—produce a progressive and rapid saponification of the fatty tissues that uselessly burden the body. The fat is transformed into soapy water, which is gradually eliminated by the natural channels. It solidifies a bit during extrusion and may take the form of soap bars or candles. A very large man can produce three packages of twelve candles in the typical model for his personal use, along with eighteen to twenty soaps and a little bottle of glycerin for skin care.

An overweight person can thus become a real source of domestic income. It's a treasure that can be exploited in man, just as one has done up to the present with bears and whales. This utilization also has the great advantage of returning the individual to normal proportions. For our doctors, this treatment presents a very simple solution. It will come as no surprise to those familiar with the miracles of modern science, but no doubt it will inflame the public's imagination.

Obviously, and we mention this for the sake of completeness, the saponification of fatty tissues has the disadvantage of making the flesh droop and sag, but unwanted wrinkles can be avoided by introducing starch into the body and giving it a good iron.

An infestation of insects in the stomach, that is, living and normally constituted insects—it's a case that piqued the curiosity of the Academy of Medicine. Compresses, surgical instruments, these are unwanted objects found in the stomach—but insects? Why not mice or rats? Their consternation was calmed at the last session, when it was made known that they were merely butterflies.

The medical profession, already so overcrowded, is about to draw even more recruits among people one would not expect to be called to medicine: the blind. Next year, it's been announced that several new *Blind Doctors for Shy Clients* will be hired. It seems that many people are reassured by this infirmity who otherwise would never dare to expose their ills. It also seems that the diagnoses made by blind doctors aren't at all inferior to those made by most of their peers.

Given the age limits imposed on admission to our primary schools and the ever more rapid and extensive nature of the education given to children, no one should be surprised to learn of the strange *Intrauterine Instruction* experiments being carried out on future newborns by the Laboratory of Psychological Physiology. It seems that a micro-phonograph can be used to instill basic notions in future children, allowing them to babble important vocabulary words as soon as they enter the world.

By gaining several months, its hoped that children who receive this training will be able to pass their college entrance exams a year earlier.

It's a discovery worthy of our era. For further details, we direct our readers to the very complete program of the *Fetal School*, which the Laboratory of Psychological Physiology will provide for free upon request.

Every day our modern surgeons accomplish real miracles. Their skill surpasses our wildest imaginings. But it must be recognized that little by little their daily practice renders their gestures automatic, and that their attention is often elsewhere, with unfortunate errors as a result. People are speaking in hushed tones about a terrible distraction that cost a patient their life in a large Parisian hospital.

It was during an extremely simple operation. The surgeon just had to cut off a finger, just one little finger, and one might initially think that even if such an operation ended in an accident, it wouldn't be a matter of any seriousness. After having cut off the finger, the surgeon should have disposed of the amputated member and sent the patient to their room, as is customary. Owing to

GASTON DE PAWLOWSKI

a terrible level of distraction, *he kept the finger and discarded the patient*. Unfortunately, by the time he recognized his error, it was already too late.

Everyday life is certainly full of absurdities.

TRANSLATOR'S NOTES

1. Diets high in sugar cause an increase in uric acid levels.

2. Prizes for humanitarian achievements awarded by the Académie Française, sometimes considered to be a forerunner of the Nobel Prize.

3. The joke here being that there were no French electors.

4. A stripped bond (*coupon détaché*) is a debt instrument whose principal has been separated from its coupon aka interest payments.

5. Bouvard and Pécuchet are the main characters of Flaubert's novel of the same name. The two court clerks move to the countryside and complete a series of disastrous projects drawing on various branches of knowledge.

6. George Auriol was a French poet and artist who also edited a satirical magazine, *Le Chat Noir*, associated with the famed cabaret.

7. The Félibrige was a cultural society for promoting Occitan languages and literature.

8. Also known as a truck, a *bogie* is the framework attached to the bottom of a modular vehicle, to which the wheels and axles are connected.

9. Atropine was used as an early anesthetic, as well as by women from ancient Egypt all the way to early twentieth-century Paris to dilate their pupils for cosmetic effect.

10. Accommodation is the process by which the eye changes optical power to focus on varying distances.

11. Oxalic acid was a household cleaner.

12. Mercury chloride, also archaically known as corrosive sublimate, was used to sterilize wounds but is no longer employed because of its mercury content.

13. Santé Prison, in the 14th arrondissement, was opened in 1867.

14. An opisimeter is a device for measuring curved lines by rolling a notched wheel along the line and counting the notches passed.

15. Chatterton and Cambouis: adhesive tape and oil, respectively.

16. Papier d'Arménie: a type of French incense made of strips of paper coated in benzoin resin.

17. Laroche is a train station in Megennes, midway between Paris and Dijon.

18. Xavier de Maistre (1763–1852) authored *Voyage around My Room*, a book about a man imprisoned in his room written as if it were a travel narrative.

19. The *Redoutable* was a French warship launched in 1791, best known for killing Vice Admiral Horatio Nelson at the Battle of Trafalgar.

20. The Château de Villette is a hunting manor outside of Paris.

21. The letter "w" rarely occurs in French and foreign words beginning with the letter are often mispronounced as if they began with a "v."

22. Lean gas is formed by the incomplete combustion of coal.

23. In 1968, this single department was divided into Paris, Hauts-de-Seine, Seine-Saint-Denis, and Val-de-Marne.

24. Cour des Miracles: Paris slums so called because beggars who faked illness or injury to earn more money during the day cast off their disabilities when returning home at night.

25. The *Maison du Vase Brisé* is a reference to Prudhomme's poem "The Broken Vase."

26. Sir Richard Wallace (1818–1890) was a British philanthropist and temperance activist who funded the constructions of so-called Wallace fountains on Paris's busiest streets, to give the poor free access to clean water after the destruction of many of the aqueducts.

27. The Chamber of Deputies is the legislative assembly of the French Parliament.

28. The Bureau des Longitudes is a French scientific institution, which, among other things, synchronized clocks around the world in the nineteenth century.

29. Slug syrup is a real treatment made by dissolving red slugs in sugar and adding alcohol.

30. Collodion is a thick solution often used to hold surgical dressings in place.

31. Taenia is a genus of tapeworms.

NOTES ON IMAGES

Doug Skinner has contributed to *Fortean Times*, *Cabinet*, *Nickelodeon*, *Weirdo*, *Fate*, *Black Scat Review*, *Strange Attractor Journal*, and other magazines. Among his books are *The Snowman Three Doors Down*, *Sleepytime Cemetery*, *Nominata*, and translations of Alphonse Allais, Charles Cros, Alfred Jarry, Pierre-Corneille Blessebois, Giovanni Battista Nazari, and Luigi Russolo.

Amanda DeMarco is a writer and translator based in Berlin.

IMAGING SCIENCE